The Abingdon
Preaching Annual
2025

The Abingdon
Preaching
Annual

2025

Planning Sermons
for Fifty-Two Sundays

Charley Reeb, General Editor

Abingdon Press
Nashville

THE ABINGDON PREACHING ANNUAL 2025:
PLANNING SERMONS FOR FIFTY-TWO SUNDAYS

Copyright © 2024 by Abingdon Press

ISBN 978-1-7910-3228-9

Scripture quotations unless noted otherwise are from the Common English Bible. Copyright © 2011 by the Common English Bible. All rights reserved. Used by permission. www.CommonEnglishBible.com.

Scripture quotations marked NRSVUE are from the New Revised Standard Version, Updated Edition. Copyright © 2021 National Council of Churches of Christ in the United States of America. Used by permission. All rights reserved worldwide.

MANUFACTURED IN THE UNITED STATES OF AMERICA

Contents

Contents

🌿 = Sunday in Lent   ☻ = Sunday of Advent

Preface

The Abingdon Preaching Annual is a resource that helps equip preachers who earnestly desire for their sermons to be used by God to touch the hearts and lives of people. This annual is filled with rich interpretations, keen insights, and prophetic guidance that will empower lectionary preachers to prepare inspiring sermons week after week.

Another valuable resource for preachers is ministrymatters.com. This site contains a wealth of instruction and inspiration for sermons and preaching. Visit the site and explore all the ways you can enhance your preaching ministry and increase your effectiveness in the pulpit.

Many thanks to the gifted team of editors at Abingdon Press for helping to bring this resource to life.

Charley Reeb
General Editor

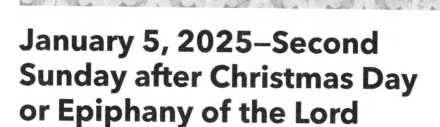

January 5, 2025–Second Sunday after Christmas Day or Epiphany of the Lord

Jeremiah 31:7-14; Psalm 147:12-20; Ephesians 1:3-14;
John 1:(1-9), 10-18; Isaiah 60:1-6; Psalm 72:1-7, 10-14;
Ephesians 3:1-12; Matthew 2:1-12

Cyndi McDonald

Preacher to Preacher Prayer

Thank you, Father, Son, and Holy Spirit, for the gift of life and your overflowing love. When I am weary, remind me that your calling is not meant to be a burden but a source of great joy in making room for others in your joyful fellowship. Amen.

Ideas for Preaching on Ephesians 3:1-12

These first few epistles and gospel scriptures suggest a sermon series titled "God Is Love," with themes exploring how God's love is reflected in action, including "Love Makes Room," "Love Shows Up," "Love Takes Risks," and "Love Never Fails."

Paul describes in Ephesians that God's plan from the beginning was that all people would be made alive through Jesus Christ (2:11). With Jesus Christ, people can have boldness and confident access to God (3:12). To the surprise of Paul and Jewish Christians, these promises were for both Jew and Gentile.

Paul, who was once fervent in his adherence to Jewish law and customs (Acts 22:3), has become equally passionate about welcoming Gentiles. He is amazed to discover that preaching to the Gentiles is a gift of grace given to him (3:8) and that God uses the church to reveal his eternal plan (3:10). We are created in the image of a God who makes room for creatures and people. We are most like the trinitarian image of God when we make room for others as a community.

Bringing the Text to Life

- Do you have a story about making room for an unwanted pet? I often begin by asking whether anyone wants a cat. We are dog people, not cat people, so of course, a malnourished cat showed up at our doorstep. Did I say we are dog people? When I expressed my reservations about adopting a cat, she reminded me of the words of the great philosopher Stephen Stills: "Love the one you're with." To our surprise, making room for this troublemaker brought immense joy.

- Do you know any families who have taken in foster or adopted children? When their older children could be more independent, a couple in our church decided to expand their family by flying to China to adopt a baby girl. Despite her health problems and being unwanted in her culture, they made room in their hearts and home for her. When they returned, they explained that they simply had more love to give.

- For a children's sermon, set a "reserved" sign on the Holy Communion table, like in restaurants. Don't be surprised if they are upset by the sign, especially if the church regularly invites all to be part of the meal. Let them tear the "reserved" sign into small pieces; they'll love throwing confetti on people in the pews and telling those present there's room for everyone at Jesus's table. I anticipated adverse reactions when one of them approached a ninety-five-year-old matriarch who was apt to complain about anything new in worship (such as the United Methodist hymnals). To my surprise, she walked around the sanctuary collecting confetti, took these home, and placed them in a bowl on her nightstand to remember God's love.

Ideas for Preaching on Matthew 2:1-12

This week's suggested theme from the lectionary scriptures is "Love Makes Room." The story of the Magi following a star may seem comforting, but for Matthew's Jewish church community, it was a surprising revelation that God welcomes even unsavory Gentiles. In today's world, to whom do we need to reach out? If we were to pray for God to send us those unwanted by others, how might God answer?

In what ways can the Magi's story inspire us to invite others into our lives intentionally? Love makes room through purposeful invitations. God doesn't simply wait for individuals to stumble upon the manger. Instead, God leads the Magi who are already seeking and invites them through a radiant star.

Although carols and stories describe three Magi, we don't know the exact number of people, only the three types of gifts. However, what's more important to note is that the Magi didn't undertake this long journey alone; they traveled together. They even devised a plan to avoid Herod on their way home. While people often say that blood is thicker than water, the church teaches us that baptismal water is strong enough to connect us to Jesus and one another. If we learned anything from the COVID-19 pandemic, we need one another. Sometimes, the most faithful thing we can do is to make room for traveling companions and encourage one another to put one foot in front of the other.

Bringing the Text to Life

- In preparation for Holy Communion, invite the congregation to bring bread for a nearby food pantry as "gifts for the newborn king." Encourage them to bring their usual: hotdog and hamburger buns, shells for Taco Tuesday, bagels, and cornbread mix. Place these on the communion table as a visible demonstration of differences and God's desire to bless all. Like the magi who were blessed by the opportunity to witness a world-changing event, they could not help but respond with gifts. When we recognize our blessings, true thankfulness will pour out on others.

- Tell the story of Grandmother Mattie Rigsby in *Walking Across Egypt*.[1] After reading the parable of the sheep and goats, Mattie decides to make room in her life for juveniles at a nearby detention center. Her family is appalled by her reluctance to report an escaped teenager who appears at her home. After a hilarious debate about the worthiness of this teen, Mattie's son argues that she has done enough for the teen. He asks, "Doesn't the Bible say when to stop?" Her answer: "No. Not that I know of." There is no end to God's love and the desire for God to make room for everyone in the new community of love.

Notes

January 12, 2025–Baptism of the Lord, First Sunday after the Epiphany

Isaiah 43:1-7; Psalm 29; **Acts 8:14-17; Luke 3:15-17, 21-22**

Cyndi McDonald

Preacher to Preacher Prayer

Holy Spirit, who once hovered over the waters of creation and baptism, be present now. Show up in the preparation. Show up when we gather for worship.

Ideas for Preaching Luke 3:15-17, 21-22

This week's suggested theme in the sermon series is "Love Shows Up." Jesus shows up with the crowds gathered at the Jordan River. He does not need the baptism of repentance that John preaches. Instead, Jesus shows up and joins those in the river because he cares about those who long for a new start.

Immediately before the lectionary passage, John preaches to "you children of snakes" that they cannot base their faith on their heritage as descendants of Abraham (v. 7). Instead, God can make sons and daughters out of the stones. This is excellent news for those of us with rock-hard hearts. God doesn't need Abrahamic DNA but wants Abrahamic faith. Where do we place our trust? In ourselves? Our possessions? Our jobs? Where we place our trust determines to whom we belong.

God speaks of family, sonship, in Jesus's baptism, and this language continues today as we acknowledge our identity as beloved children of God during our baptisms. The barriers that separate us from the divine realm are torn apart, and we hear God's voice declaring, "This is my son. This is my daughter." Love shows up, and we are transformed.

Bringing the Text to Life

- Invite the congregation to respond to hearing God's word by touching the water in the baptismal font and giving thanks that they are baptized. Pour a few precious drops from a crystal or china creamer into the font, explaining that this is water from the Jordan River (available online at Amazon and other retailers). Then, pour a substantial amount from a plain pitcher, explaining that this is from the kitchen sink. In our baptism, the extraordinary Jesus, who showed up at the Jordan River, meets us in our ordinary kitchen-sink lives.

- How does love show up in your congregation? Do you have a Fran— she always beats me to the hospital when I visit a congregant. She loves her church family and is the first to show up when someone is in need. Does your church show up with meals to support those who grieve? Or to parents with new babies? Stephen Ministers shows up to listen. Volunteers show up at school to tutor at-risk kids. These are ways of living out our baptism; Jesus shows up for others through us.

- Do you have a personal experience of how love has shown up in your own life? If not, tell a story from a favorite book or movie in which someone shows love by showing up: In *Home Alone*, Kate McCallister refuses to wait, travels multiple connecting flights, and even accepts a ride with a polka band, wanting to show up and be with Kevin. In *A Man Called Ove*, the neighbor Parvaneh persists through Ove's initial resistance and grumpiness and shows up repeatedly.[2]

- If emphasizing baptism as a time of new beginning, describe the butterfly metamorphosis process. Caterpillars don't become butterflies by growing wings and legs. Instead, the process is much more comprehensive. The caterpillar secretes enzymes in the cocoon that dissolve the creature into a liquid. Change occurs at the cellular level. If God can transform rocks into children, then how might God transform them into new creations in Christ through baptism?

- Michelangelo's painting of God reaching out to Adam on the Sistine Chapel ceiling can symbolize the divine connection made through baptism. For adults or confirmands affirming their baptism, this is a moment when we repent and reach out to God; God has already shown up and reached out to us.

Ideas for Preaching on Acts 8:14-17

This is one of many examples in Acts of the Holy Spirit appearing to Gentiles. Love shows up to people the Jewish disciples did not expect, such as these historic enemies. Remember, Jesus's disciples wanted to call down fire on a Samaritan town (Luke 9:54)!

Belief and baptism are accompanied by manifestations of the Holy Spirit throughout Acts. However, in this situation, it is necessary for representatives from Jerusalem to be present and see that God is working among the Samaritans. Do the Samaritans need to know that their Jerusalem brethren will show up for them? Or should the Jerusalem church understand that they have a responsibility to show up without any limitations as to person or place?

Bringing the Text to Life

- Luke's Gospel and Acts celebrate Jesus and the Holy Spirit showing up. If you remember your baptism in worship, consider placing in the font red glass stones, like those available at craft stores, for congregants to take as a remembrance. Red is a Pentecostal color and also a symbol of the Holy Spirit. Encourage your congregation to remember that just as the Holy Spirit lights on Jesus, the Holy Spirit is present in their baptism. Place the stones where they can remember that God has not stopped showing up in the world; God is showing up in them and through them.

- The Hebrew and Greek words for spirit (*ruach* and *pneuma*) can also be translated as breath, such as when God shapes a lump of dirt into the form of a human and breathes in life. Use this understanding of the Spirit as breath to give thanks for the gift of the Holy Spirit in baptism. Specifically, lead the congregation in breath prayer, in which they will breathe in a phrase and breathe out another. Instruct the community to close their eyes. Breathe in. They may feel various hurts in their bodies or a little tension from recent days. Breathe in. As long as you are breathing, there's more right with you than wrong. Breathe out. God's spirit is breathing in and out with you, giving life. Challenge the church to start each day with a breath prayer: Breathe in. "Holy Spirit, you are with me." Breathe out. "Holy Spirit, bless this day."

Notes

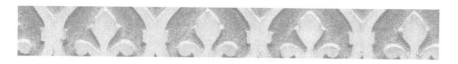

January 19, 2025–Second Sunday after the Epiphany

Isaiah 62:1-5; Psalm 36:5-10; **1 Corinthians 12:1-11; John 2:1-11**

Cyndi McDonald

Preacher to Preacher Prayer

Creator God, giver of life, we thank you for this day. We trust you to give us what we most need, even if not what we ask for. May we use your gifts in ways that honor you. Amen.

Ideas for Preaching on John 2:1-11

Continuing in the sermon series, this week's sermon series theme is "Love Notices." In the Gospel of John, Jesus's first miracle is turning water into wine. This first of seven signs reveals his glory and encourages his followers to believe in him. When two of his disciples ask where he is staying, Jesus invites them to "come and see." Their first stop is an ordinary home in Galilee, and on the third day, they attend a wedding celebration in nearby Cana.

When the wine runs out, Mary notices and approaches Jesus for help. What better description for prayer than describing a situation and expecting God to act? It is unfair that a couple should be labeled "incapable of providing" for the rest of their lives. Instead, they will begin with extraordinary abundance.

Love notices is only the beginning of the story. As Joanna Harader notes, miracles often involve the hard work of those in the vicinity.[3] Jesus does not say, "Let there be wine," but involves those present. Servants lug 120 gallons of water to the six jars and then serve the guests. Later, Jesus notices a hungry crowd and instructs the disciples to serve loaves and fish to five thousand people. At the tomb of Lazarus, Jesus orders mourners to push the stone away and then to unbind Lazarus.

Bringing the Text to Life

* What do we need to notice? What situations do we need to describe to God and expect action? This Sunday, lean into the Martin Luther King, Jr. holiday. What would today's Mary notice and name regarding recent racial injustices that do not reflect the world God desires?

- When have you seen a miraculous ministry in your church? Did it begin with someone noticing? When I served at Barnesville UMC, a high-school basketball star was injured and in a wheelchair for months after a series of operations. Her family declared it a miracle that the church could provide a ramp while she was in a wheelchair. The miracle began when someone with the "gift of noticing" recognized the need for temporary ramps during hospice care or following surgery. Others put in hours searching online for used ramps, then traveling across state lines to pick them up. Still more showed up to install and then replace these ramps as needed. We may be so used to the presence of church ministries that we forget they are received as a miraculous answer to prayer, a sign that glorifies God and encourages trust in Jesus.

- For a children's sermon, describe how Jesus continues to turn the ordinary into the extraordinary. Invite a quilter or knitter to show how bits of fabric or string are made into a beautiful quilt or shawl. If your church has a compassion ministry that feeds families after a funeral, have a volunteer explain how they take ordinary flour, sugar, and eggs to bake a cake, bringing comfort and reminding them that they are not alone. Give children ordinary paper, crayons, and stickers and charge them to make cards for shut-ins. At the end of the service, have them bring these to the prayer rail and pray for those who will receive the cards.

- While the steward recognizes the change in wine quality, most miss the miracle. Tell the Midrash story of the Israelites crossing the Red Sea. Reuven and Shimon scowl and grumble about the mud on their sandals as they walk. They compare the mud to the slime pits of Egypt. "What is the difference?" complained Shimon. "Mud here; mud there; it is all the same." They never notice they are walking in a miracle.[4] Encourage people to see the miracles around them by challenging them to list 120 reasons to be grateful—twenty per day for the next six days. Bring your list next Sunday! Look up instead of at the mud! Love notices. Can they notice the ways God blesses each day?

Ideas for Preaching on 1 Corinthians 12:1-11

Love notices. Unfortunately, some in the Corinthian church only pay attention to how they are superior to others, suggesting they have a higher spiritual status due to their unique abilities.

Paul argues against any hierarchy, emphasizing that the Holy Spirit gifts everyone. By calling these "gifts" rather than skills or rewards, he implies that these abilities are not earned but grace. A gift of prophecy or miracle-working signifies God's greatness, not that of the receiver.

Using the trinitarian names of God, Jesus, and the Holy Spirit, Paul reminds us that they act as one. Further, the Holy Spirit guides and empowers people to devote their lives to Jesus Christ, proclaiming Jesus as Lord. What a contrast to those who argue their spiritual gifts are a sign of superiority. I imagine Paul sarcastically asking whether his readers know more than the Holy Spirit, who directs attention to Jesus rather than herself.

Paul's list of spiritual gifts is incomplete; perhaps he listed those most valued by the community. The real test is not which gift is received but whether it is used for the common good. Does it demonstrate compassion for those who are often ignored? Does it contribute to the betterment of the community?

Bringing the Text to Life

Lists of spiritual gifts are often accompanied by surveys and invitations to look within to identify your gifts. But love notices. Pay attention to how God is working in the lives of others. Look for the gifts shown in others.

- This is an excellent week to commission new leaders in the church. They have sought to use their gifts for the common good. Ask them to come forward and kneel and have others lay hands. Ask the congregation to lift hands towards them and participate in the prayers.

- One of my mentors, a retired minister, frequently visited churches to encourage their support for missions. He always paid careful attention to the prayer requests made during the service or listed in the bulletin, saying you can tell much about a church from their prayers. Do they pray for those beyond the church? For the common good of all?

- Unlike the church in Corinth, divisions today are less likely to be about spiritual gifts than about who is right or righteous. Read Ann Weems' touching story "Stars for the Righteous," in which a little girl is challenged to show love for a friend rather than earning Sunday School prizes.[5]

Notes

January 26, 2025–Third Sunday after the Epiphany

Nehemiah 8:1-3, 5-6, 8-10; Psalm 19; **1 Corinthians 12:12-31a;** *Luke 4:14-21*

Cyndi McDonald

Preacher to Preacher Prayer

Dear Lord, thank you for not waiting for me to get everything right before reaching out with grace. Please help me to see others in the same way. Too often, when I meet someone, I look for gifts and skills to help the church. Instead, show me how I help them draw closer to you. Amen.

Ideas for Preaching on Luke 4:14-21

A potential theme for today's lessons is "Love Says Today." Jesus selects and reads Isaiah's prophecy that God will anoint and send a messenger declaring that this is the year of the Lord's favor. Jesus declares there is no waiting. The scripture has been fulfilled. Love says today.

You may need to remind your congregation that before the Israelites entered the promised land, areas were assigned to each tribe, ensuring enough for everyone. However, poor choices and unfortunate circumstances would lead some to lose land. Subsequent generations might have insufficient resources. Some will be misfortunate and enslave themselves or family members to pay debts. A Jubilee year every fifty years would free those in bondage, forgive debts, and return the land to its original allocations where everyone has enough.

Baptism includes receiving the Holy Spirit.[6] We join Jesus in fulfilling today's scripture, anointed and sent with the good news of the Jubilee era Jesus began. We join in Jesus's prayer, "on earth as it is in heaven." If we know that there will be no tears in eternity and wrongs will be set right, how do we make it so now? Love says today.

Bringing the Text to Life

- Matthew Myer Boulton defines *fulfilled* as embodied. A shirt sleeve can only be appreciated when an arm slides in and fills it.[7] How do we see Jesus embodying the Jubilee promise?

- What waiting games do we play rather than embody God's promises? In "tit for tat," we repay with what we receive. We could instead live in God's grace, extending this to others.

- When have you seen God work through someone unwilling to wait? As a newborn, our son Matt stopped breathing when asleep, which required an apnea monitor. We stopped attending church, unwilling to leave him in the nursery, as he could need CPR if he napped. No one called, and we felt abandoned. Five years later, expecting our second child, we renewed our intention to raise our children in the church. This time, our experience was radically different. When Debbie (name changed) heard we would not attend often over the next six months because Mark had the same condition, she took an infant CPR class and learned to use the apnea monitor. She would enter the nursery on Sunday mornings and say, "I am not here to work in the nursery; I am here to care for Mark," and then play or walk with Mark. Love said today rather than make us wait six months to find our place in our new church family.

- In the movie *Just Mercy*, Bryan Stevenson faces obstacles to bring justice for Walter McMillian, an innocent man sentenced to death. Stevenson and the Equal Initiative Project he founded are not content to wait for the justice system to correct itself but to work for reform today.[8]

Ideas for Preaching on 1 Corinthians 12:12-31a

Paul continues to address the divisions within the Corinthian church, where some think they do not need others. What a tragedy to tell someone, "I do not need you." However, we imply that when ranking and valuing gifts. Suggesting that gifts are unnecessary will be heard as you are not needed. Do not hesitate to affirm the gifts of others. Love says today.

Paul describes two ways in which God hampers divisions. First, no one person has every gift needed. We must depend on one another.

Second, God acts to eliminate divisions and ensure mutual concern. Rather than get bogged down in presentable versus shameful body parts, remember that when we rank gifts, we get the ranking backward. The preacher could point out that when you come to a "so that" in scripture, as in verse 25, slow down and read carefully. See how God addresses divisions and builds mutual concern.

In "Letter from Birmingham Jail," Martin Luther King, Jr. wrote that a more significant threat to the civil rights movement than the Ku Klux Klan was white Christians who discouraged actions and urged waiting for a "more convenient" time.[9] Who do we hesitate to support, waiting for the convenient time? Love says today.

Bringing the Text to Life

* Do you have a story of the first becoming last and the last first? I often ask fellow students about their experiences in healthy churches during seminary. One international student shared that elders were revered in his tradition, given the most important church titles and roles. At one time, his church had been unhealthy, as elders were given positions out of fear. If overlooked, they could leave and take an entire family with them. Several elders colluded and declined the "important" positions, asking for the least honored tasks. They shifted the church culture to see great honor in chores like taking out the trash and collecting bulletins after a worship service.

* Most congregations think of themselves as welcoming and friendly. It is easy to be friendly when you first meet someone. However, as you get to know their quirks, it can grow difficult. When has your church overcome divisions caused by a difficult person? During the COVID-19 pandemic, one family rejected safety protocols, even near at-risk individuals, causing dissension. When the family contracted COVID-19 and could not work, church members immediately forgot their dissensions and supported the family with meals and money for bills.

Notes

February 2, 2025–Fourth Sunday after the Epiphany

Jeremiah 1:4-10; Psalm 71:1-6; **1 Corinthians 13:1-13; Luke 4:21-30**

Cyndi McDonald

Preacher to Preacher Prayer

Dear Lord, what grief we have known. We've seen communities we expected to hold together instead fall apart. Heal the grief with your never-failing, never-ending love, that we might show love to others.

Ideas for Preaching on Luke 4:21-30

The "God Is Love" series concludes with the theme "Love Never Fails." We continue last week's depiction of Jesus in his hometown synagogue when he reads the Isaiah scroll and proclaims its fulfillment that day.

Luke links the lack of miracles with stories that enrage the hometown crowd. They don't want to hear about Elijah providing unlimited flour and oil for the Gentile widow of Zarephath (1 Kings 17:7-16); they want plentiful food for their widows and the people of Galilee. They don't want to hear about Elisha healing the leprosy of the enemy General Naaman; they want healing for their families and soldiers.

Perhaps this is the moment when someone points out that Jesus omitted the "day of God's vengeance" (NSRV, KJV, NAS, and other translations) when reading Isaiah 61:2. How might the fulfillment of God's promises require our letting go of the desire for retribution?

Jesus stays true to God's long-held desire to bless all families of the earth (Genesis 12:3). Love never fails, staying focused on the true purpose. God's grace and love must transcend economic differences, social status, and power structures.

As a card-carrying "people pleaser," I avoid words that cause conflict or departure. In contrast, Jesus disappoints others to focus on his mission. Later in the chapter, he disappears rather than using the gathering crowds as an opportunity for fundraising or as a platform. More important is to spend time in prayer and continue the journey. He was sent to proclaim the good news of the kingdom of God to other cities and people (4:42-43).

Bringing the Text to Life

- Drew Hart describes both how hate harms the person and how the capacity to love can transform the person. The kingdom of God is not brought about by vengeance, which perpetuates cycles of violence. Alternatively, love can convert social and political enemies to struggle for the kingdom of God. Chapter 9 describes God's never-failing, never-ending love with God sending Jonah to the enemy Nineveh.[1] Remind your church of your primary purpose. If you have a mission statement related to making disciples of Jesus Christ for the transformation of the world, explain how the goal affected a recent decision like the church budget, a calendar decision, or the ministry of the church.

- In the *Ted Lasso* television series, Ted describes his goal as "helping these young fellas [the players] be the best versions of themselves on and off the field." The football-crazy fans who want a winning season or at least to avoid relegation don't appreciate Ted's goals, but Ted keeps his focus and endures criticism, name-calling, and player conflicts.[2]

Ideas for Preaching on 1 Corinthians 13:1-13

The preacher may consider 1 Corinthians 13 problematic in its familiarity and beauty. What can be added? Turn the attention from a familiar reading for newlyweds to the axiom that God is love (1 John 4:8). God's character, vision, and activity center around love.

Unfortunately, wrong ideas about God can distort our understanding of what it means to love God and love others. What misunderstandings about God lead the Corinthians to rank one another's gifts rather than to see one another as images of God? What misunderstandings encourage factions about whether to follow Paul, Apollos, or Peter?

In his book on spiritual formation, Christopher Hall describes the beginning of Christian spiritual formation as ridding oneself of wrong understandings about God. Every distorted image he provides contradicts one of the descriptions of love given in 1 Corinthians 13.[3] A fundamental understanding of Wesleyan spiritual formation is that we grow more perfect in love, as seen in the UMC ordination question, "Do you expect to be made perfect in love in this life?"[4] This does not mean that the Christian never sins or makes mistakes but that the Christian is motivated by love. Through grace, we are shaped so that our natural response is love.

Bringing the Text to Life

- Print or make slides of 1 Corinthians 13:4-8a with blanks for the word *love*: such as "____ is patient" "____ is kind," "____ isn't jealous," "____ endures all things," and "____ never fails." Most people are comfortable with filling in the blanks with "Jesus." What about God? Do they see God as kind, patient, putting up with all things, unhappy with injustice? Encourage them to rank how well their image of God reflects each characteristic of love. What ideas about God might need to be challenged?

- An Internet search of "Soup Nazi" will generate numerous clips from *Seinfeld* in which an obnoxious chef serves the most amazing soup. Unfortunately, he is the opposite of the characteristics described in 1 Corinthians 13. "No soup for you" if you allow someone to break in line. "No soup for you" if you don't order quickly. "No soup for you" if you ask for bread that others receive. One mistake and you will never get soup again. What if we wrongly imagined God as the Grace Nazi? You mess up? No grace for you. Ever. Are there times when we act as though God withholds grace? A though God is impatient with us?

- Christopher Hall, who taught spiritual formation at the college level, names some of the common images of God described by his students: Demanding Parent (such as that of Norman Bates's mom in *Psycho*), Divine Drill Instructor (disciplines weak failures to whip them into shape), Cosmic Monster (an untrustworthy God who permits evil), and Indulgent Grandparent (content with kids having fun and not caring about sin). Which of these do you see in your congregation? How might knowing God as the love described in 1 Corinthians 13 counter each distorted view?[5] Love is kind, which shares the same root word as *kin*.[6] Someone is kind when they treat another like kin or family. Contrast telling a guest, "This is where you will sleep; here are some clean towels," with a family who knows that there is a place for them no matter their mistakes.

Notes

February 9, 2025–Fifth Sunday after the Epiphany

*Isaiah 6:1-8, (9-13); Psalm 138; **1 Corinthians 15:1-11; Luke 5:1-11***

Cynthia D. Weems

Preacher to Preacher Prayer

Gracious God, thank you for the opportunity to proclaim your salvific work. May our words be instruments of your grace and power. Amen.

Ideas for Preaching on 1 Corinthians 15:1-11

The clarity of this passage is admirable. Paul retells the whole story of what transpires in the four Gospels in just a few sentences. He practically bullet points Jesus's life, death, and resurrection. Then he goes on to list how the story of Jesus spread. He owns his own complicity in persecuting the early followers of Jesus. Then he gives himself credit for working harder than all the others to proclaim the good news (with God's grace, of course).

Paul, writing to the Corinthian believers, is convinced that the message most needed is a simple and direct one. He wants these followers to get back to the basics of the faith and stop messing around with bickering and disagreements. Returning them to a straightforward, uncomplicated message will surely help this community to get back on track.

A question for Christ followers today might be where we include ourselves in the larger narrative of sharing the story of the life, death, and resurrection of Jesus. If we were to simply state the trajectory of Christian history as Paul did, where would our own lives and contributions land? Are there specific ways that our lives share the joy and hope of the life, death, and resurrection of Jesus?

In Paul's case, he takes great pride in emphasizing the saving work of Jesus and acknowledging his role in sharing that work with the world. He is convicted by the power of salvation. It feels contagious in his writing, and one can imagine what the hearers were feeling as they listened to this letter being read aloud in the congregation. As preachers, we hope to have that same contagious spirit in our weekly proclamations. Lay persons also have ample opportunities to share the gospel in contagious ways. Help your listeners to remember the importance of being that person who shares the gospel in word and deed.

A preacher might do well to ask if salvation through Jesus's life, death, and resurrection is a set a bullet points we are passionate about today. Do we see the mark of God's grace in our lives such that we are working daily to proclaim the good news of salvation to all through our hope, joy, abounding love, and compassion?

Bringing the Text to Life

- Use an illustration of a circuit-riding preacher in frontier America. How was his life and preaching similar to the simple proclamation in Paul's letter to the Corinthians?

- The Greek verb *sozo* means saved, made whole, restored, healed, delivered, preserved. Does this help us understand why Paul might have been so passionate about salvation through Jesus?

- Use a simple image of the cross.

Ideas for Preaching on Luke 5:1-11

This passage presents numerous opportunities for preaching. Perhaps reflecting on recent events in the life of your congregation and the particular context of current events in the world at the time of preaching will help you discern the direction to take.

Interactions between Simon Peter and Jesus are always fodder for good preaching! This passage is no different. There is trust and intimacy in their relationship. Yet, Jesus always wants to push Simon Peter to grow deeper in that trust. In this passage, Jesus literally invites Simon Peter into deeper water. Jesus is often inviting us into deeper water too. By doing this, Jesus challenges us to leave our fears behind and move into greater faith and hope. Jesus reminds us that we can do difficult things, make hard decisions, and still be standing on the other side. Jesus reminds us that he will always be with us, even when there is fear, depth, darkness, and uncertainty. In fact, might Jesus be in the deep waters already and asking us to come and journey with him there?

What does heading out into the deep look like in our lives? What do the shallow waters feel like, and how do they convince us that this is where we need to remain? As a pastor, you are able to name circumstances in the lives of your congregation that fit into these categories. Often people will resist engaging in a Bible study because they are fearful of what they might learn if they dig deeper into the sacred scriptures. Parents often seek to remain in the shallow end of life with their teenagers because the deep end might require learning hard realities about the complexities of teen living today—such as mental health struggles, complicated friendships, and risky behaviors. Couples will remain in the shallow end of a marriage rather than dive deeply into their hopes and dreams or the truth of their disappointments. A person might stay in the same job for too long rather than take a chance with a new challenge in the deep end.

Here enters the net. The invitation to cast the net widely is an invitation to bounty. It is an invitation to trust Jesus to take us places where the fear and uncertainty might result in physical, spiritual, emotional, or literal bounty. Simon Peter's response reminds us that it is hard for us to accept the bounty of Jesus at times. "Get back!" We feel unworthy to receive it or guilty for having doubted it. The bounty is given freely as we walk closely with Jesus. To be clear, most of life's hard work does not result in a relatively easy catch of fish. In fact, we often find ourselves in a heap of grief and uncertainty when we follow Jesus into the deep waters. Making hard life decisions can result in hard realities. Yet, the deep water is ultimately a place of hope.

Bringing the Text to Life

- Recount an experience of a child moving from shallow water to deep water in a swimming pool or an adult taking the added risk of scuba diving in deep waters.

- Display a large net. Ask people to imagine what "bounty" looks like in their life today. Ask if they are willing to go into the deep with Jesus to receive it.

- Consider closing with the hymn "Lord, You Have Come to the Lakeshore" in English or Spanish.

Notes

February 16, 2025–Sixth Sunday after the Epiphany

*Jeremiah 17:5-10; **Psalm 1**; 1 Corinthians 15:12-20; **Luke 6:17-26***

Cynthia D. Weems

Preacher to Preacher Prayer

Almighty God, grant your wisdom to the preparation and sharing of these texts this week. May the blessings represented in them become blessings to our hearers. Amen.

Ideas for Preaching on Psalm 1

This relatively brief psalm can be a delight to preach. It empowers the faithful to demonstrate their love of God by actively doing those things that will help their lives to flourish rather than participating in those things that will cause them to sin. This psalm can read as a very simple set of instructions—do this, but don't do this! We know that life is not quite as simple as that. However, the psalmist does anticipate a willing heart to seek the good and turn away from evil.

On this note, a preacher might use this opportunity to lift up examples of how a person seeks the good and avoids the bad. I think it would be helpful to share everyday examples of how this works in real time. How can we choose God's instruction when responding to emails, talking with our kids, dealing with a difficult coworker, or managing an unhealthy family member? How can we choose the course of evil in those same situations where resentment, anger, gossip, spite, or jealousy can get the best of us?

The image of the tree planted by a stream of water that bears fruit at just the right time and whose leaves never fade is a lovely one. I encourage you to get as much mileage out of this while preaching as you can! A tree by a stream is in a great position to receive nourishment and offer its fruit "at just the right time." A person living by this image would receive nourishment from healthy relationships, scripture, a church home, good health, and meaningful work. That person would likely bear fruit at just the right time to benefit all others around her.

However, the impact of the image ends there, I believe. People are not stationary, and streams do dry up. The reality is that we all live, breathe, and move in the world and we cannot rely on always being in close proximity to healthy, flourishing streams of water to propel the good fruit from our branches. We do struggle to follow the good and turn away from the evil. This will help the preacher turn to practical ways and ideas to help us be as close to the life-giving stream as possible, ensuring we are doing the most we possibly can to bear good fruit through our actions, words, and decisions.

Bringing the Text to Life

* Print Psalm 1 in a way that allows parishioners to take it home with them.

* Demonstrate a very long list of instructions, even a roll of long paper, and humorously lift up that this psalm indicates that those who love the Lord recite God's instructions "day and night."

* Display an image of a tree next to a stream and compare it to one where the tree is a great distance from water.

Ideas for Preaching on Luke 6:17-26

In this text from Luke's Gospel, a tone of expectation is set for the remainder of what is known as the Sermon on the Plain. Verses 17-19 build an expectation that a preacher might be wise to explore with a congregation. It is easy to jump to the next verses, which present a portion of what we know as the Beatitudes (Matthew's version is more commonly used). Yet, it is worth spending time in the expectation of the early verses before diving into Jesus's response to that expectation.

Specifically, the hopes of the large crowd of people gathered together are named. Not only are we told the distance people have traveled to come and see Jesus, but also we are told their specific desires and outcomes: to hear Jesus, to touch Jesus, to be healed from their diseases, to rid them of their unclean spirits. The people surrounding Jesus, as is often the case, need Jesus to alleviate their very real and tangible ailments. The passage confirms that Jesus did this and that he had more to say to them beyond the healing of their many illnesses.

A beatitude is a blessing. Jesus is offering words of blessing to those gathered. Significantly, this blessing is not a result of good behavior, a job well done, a merit badge, or a task completed on time. This blessing is a gift from God. This blessing speaks to the nature of who God is and how God wants creation to experience a relationship with God.

In my United Methodist tradition, an oft used term to describe a gift that comes without strings is prevenient grace. This term refers to the nature of God and the grace that is given freely and without the expectation of reward, response, or repayment. While reading this passage from Luke and reflecting on the nature of a beatitude, I felt the tug of prevenient grace on my heart and mind. Jesus is surrounded by a crowd of followers. They will do what he asks them to do. They are desperate for a response to their various ailments, many very serious in nature. Culturally, they are inclined to believe there will be a transaction required of them in order for healing to occur. Does healing really come without a price?

Jesus chooses to bless them instead of charge them for his services. The blessing he offers is not simply the words that we have come to know as the Beatitudes. He blesses them with words that reflect how God sees their precious lives. Those who are most forgotten in this world are blessed and will be blessed. A blessing is a pronouncement that is immediate, not just pointing to a future state. When a blessing is offered in a worship service, it is a conveyance of blessing, not a promissory note for the future. In this way, Jesus blessed in real time those gathered around him and also points to a future hope in God's promises. Of course, the preacher must also address the final verses that name the reality of injustice and those who do not receive God's blessing. In this way, the sermon can and should point to modern-day examples of how the secular world and its priorities often bless or praise the opposite of who Jesus is blessing or praising.

Bringing the Text to Life

- Consider incorporating a blessing of the people into the worship service.

- Design a creative way for people to bless one another.

- Offer examples of the many transactional relationships in our lives to show the stark contrast to what Jesus is doing in this passage.

Notes

February 23, 2025–Seventh Sunday after the Epiphany

Genesis 45:3-11, 15; Psalm 37:1-11, 39-40; 1 Corinthians 15:35-38, 42-50; Luke 6:27-38

Cynthia D. Weems

Preacher to Preacher Prayer

Gracious God, impart on us all the gift of forgiveness. May the sharing of these scriptures bring forth in us the desire to share grace with others. Amen.

Ideas for Preaching on Genesis 45:3-11

Throughout the early narrative of Joseph's life, God is never mentioned. Though this passage is in the later stages of Joseph's narrative, it is worth mentioning the absence of God's name again when reflecting on chapter 45, recapping the whole story quickly for your listeners. So much has happened before arriving at these dramatic verses that it will be important to be sure the listeners are aware of all that came before this climax. The Joseph story is clearly one of the most heart-wrenching and life-giving stories in scripture.

A question that must be explored when preaching this scripture is what Joseph meant by, "You didn't send me here; it was God" (v. 8). Without exploring this fully, a whole host of shallow theological answers could be inferred by listeners. Lest the congregation come away with the popular, secular notion that "all things happen for a reason," we want to give them a greater array of theological options to combat that thinking. A good place to start is Joseph's reintroduction of God into the larger narrative.

What is clearly heard in these verses is Joseph's voice. He is now the narrator, and the way he shapes the narrative is very important. Joseph does not negate the terrible things that happened to him. Yet, he is able to acknowledge and rejoice in God's presence throughout. He is able to see the way his faithful God carried him through difficult times and offered a new way when all seemed lost. Notice Joseph does not claim that God orchestrated the story of his life. Rather, God was present with him and God was faithful, just as Joseph was faithful.

Then, significant, and perhaps the most important part for your listeners, is Joseph's very human response to his brothers who are now right in front of him and scared out of their wits. Joseph not only recounts the narrative of his life with God in the midst of it but also, in turn, responds to his brothers' evil toward him with grace and dignity. He surprises them with forgiveness, concern for their father, and immediate plans to help the family in their time of distress.

Bringing the Text to Life

- Display a quilt or describe the art of quilting. Ask persons to consider the patchwork of their lives and the places where they have felt God's presence.

- Describe briefly how a person might go about writing a memoir. Ask the congregation who would be the characters in their memoirs? Would God be one of them?

- Use any number of artistic pieces that represent Joseph's reunion with his brothers.

Ideas for Preaching on Luke 6:27-38

Preaching on this text ideally begins with a heart-to-heart with the congregation about who they are dealing with in this passage—Jesus. We are walking into the heart and mind of Jesus, and he will ask us to do things in today's passage that do not come naturally to us.

When it comes to anger or response to evil and meanness, Jesus seems to head in the other direction from where we often want to go. People might describe Jesus as someone who goes easy on bad people. They might say his instructions aren't fair as they ignore the harm done. One might argue that he makes it impossible for people to defend themselves from those who do bad things to them.

One question to ask is, "What are we defending?" Are we defending our right to respond violently to another person? Are we defending our right to our possessions? What might Jesus be asking us to defend with his response to "turn the other cheek"?

The power of Jesus does not come through brute strength but through love and compassion. The ability to offer the other cheek to someone who has just hit you takes a lot more strength, might, force, and power than landing a punch. This power comes from our hearts, not our bodies.

Jesus had many opportunities to defend himself against attacks. His credibility was attacked and he was attacked physically. Yet he always managed to defend not himself, but God. Jesus sought to defend God and God's promises for the world—even when no one else seemed to believe they were real.

Ultimately, we, too, are asked to defend God and the vision God has for the world. We are not asked by Jesus to defend ourselves or our stuff or our priorities or our bodies or even our country. We are asked by Jesus to defend God and God's dream that we live in a world where people are loved and shown love rather than hate and violence. We can do this by the way we respond to emails, texts, snide comments, being passed over for a promotion, or hearing political views or religious views with which we disagree.

This passage defies the larger culture in which we live, a culture that seeks reciprocal retaliation. This passage reminds us that we are in the business of defending God and the hope of God for this world. This is not easy, especially when the tools we are given to defend God are love, hope, honesty, and kindness rather sharp objects and weapons.

Bringing the Text to Life

- Ask the congregation to write down on a piece of paper an example of how they have been "hit" on the cheek. Then give them a way to physically leave/offer/destroy it.

- Illustrations from the book *Three Cups of Tea* by Greg Mortenson share a hopeful response to evil and harm in the world.

- Check recent newspapers for examples of retaliation through verbal or physical contact.

Notes

March 2, 2025–Transfiguration Sunday

Exodus 34:29-35; *Psalm 99; 2 Corinthians 3:12-4:2;*
Luke 9:28-36, (37-43a)

Cynthia D. Weems

Preacher to Preacher Prayer

Dear Lord, thank you for the transformation you bring to our lives through your presence and your willingness to make yourself known to us. May the reflections of my heart share the brilliance of your divine nature. Amen.

Ideas for Preaching on Exodus 34:29-35

It is common to compare the Exodus and Luke passages today because they are so similar and because they provide deep context for understanding the powerful nature of what happens with God in high places. Moses met God on Mount Sinai and came away shining. Jesus, the son of God, climbs to an elevated place and also receives a kind of shining glow. So, we may ask together as these scriptures are read publicly and transfiguration is preached, "What happened up there?"

Moses had been fasting for forty days and nights. Anyone could argue that pure hunger made him shine! We believe what happened for both Moses and Jesus was a kind of transformation. The essence of their being was not changed. Moses remained very much Moses and Jesus remained very much Jesus. But it was as if their encounter with the Almighty God set fire to them in a way that caused them to physically react. The physical reaction represented something far greater happening deep within their beings.

We experience God through these passages as the pure, dazzling light of presence, and this can be outlined briefly in the preaching moment to build a beautiful storyline of God's presence with the people of Israel. Looking back on the larger story found in Exodus, a few notable moments bookend today's passage. In chapter 24 the Lord called Moses to come to the mountain. It says, "the Lord's glorious presence settled on Mount Sinai." Then, "To the Israelites, the Lord's glorious presence looked like a blazing fire on top of the mountain" (vv. 16-17).

In today's passage from chapter 34, Moses begins to shine like a lightbulb after returning to the mountain to receive the second set of tablets with the Ten Commandments written on them. Moses is now shining from this pure, dazzling light of God's presence. Then, in chapter 40, Moses is given specific instructions for building the tabernacle. This is the place where the altar, the lamps, the oil, and the ark would be placed—all of the holy things. When the tabernacle is complete, we are told that "the cloud" covered the tabernacle and "the LORD's glorious presence filled the dwelling" (v. 34). The glory of the Lord that was once high on the mountain is now resting in the tabernacle where it would remain in the midst of the people of Israel. Moses was a key figure in the Almighty's movement from high on the mountain to right in the center of the people. How do we live with God's shining light in the center of our homes and lives?

Bringing the Text to Life

- Display an artistic image of Moses returning from Mount Sinai with "the glow."

- Ask people if they have ever encountered someone who gave the impression of beaming with the joy of God.

- Use a lightbulb or lamp to demonstrate the importance of light and compare it to God's abiding light with us.

Ideas for Preaching on Luke 9:28-36, (37-43a)

The mystery of the transfiguration is palpable in this passage from Luke's Gospel. It has elements that feel like the baptism narratives in which a uniquely powerful moment is happening between Jesus the Son and God the Creator, while there are witnesses to (somewhat) awkwardly see it all unfold. It is not surprising that any human response to the powerful moment seems flawed and imperfect. Peter, John, and James are no different.

These three disciples experienced the mystery and then wanted to do what humans often want to do: find a way to make it last. Resentful and saddened by the thought that this might be a fleeting moment, Peter suggested building monuments so they could concrete the whole thing into a perpetual remembrance. But that wasn't meant to be. There is no memorial. No marking in a physical way the experience of transfiguration. Today's passage is about the transfiguration of Christ on the mountain, and it is also about the return back down that same mountain.

Ask the congregation to consider their own profound life experiences. Ask them if they ever wanted to put it on pause and hold it in place. Even more than brief interludes, perhaps there are times in people's lives where they can name a season that due to its fullness and power and fulfilment, everything else felt like a valley after that season of life. These feelings are real and they help us to relate to the disciples who were with Jesus. They also help us to understand what Jesus might want to teach us from this passage. Jesus wanted the disciples to be able to return to the world, descend back into the earthly life fraught with challenges and carry with them the gift of experiencing that intimacy with God. Will they be able to do that? Are we able to do it?

Concluding the sermon with a series of questions about how our encounters with the holy impact our daily living could be meaningful for the congregation. How is the glory of God revealing itself in our lives and in the life of the congregation?

Bringing the Text to Life

- *When Glory, A Blessing for Transfiguration Sunday* by Jan Richardson

- Transfiguration was a class at Hogwarts according to the Harry Potter book series. The class was about changing one thing into another using a wand, charms, or spells. Talk about how this is *not* what happens in Luke's Gospel. Jesus becomes more of himself, not something different.

- Recount a "mountain top" experience in your own life or the life of someone you know well. These experiences are powerful illustrations.

Notes

March 5, 2025–Ash Wednesday

Joel 2:1-2, 12-17; Isaiah 58:1-12; Psalm 51:1-17;
2 Corinthians 5:20b-6:10; *Matthew 6:1-6, 16-21*

Chelsea Simon

Preacher to Preacher Prayer

Dear God, as we begin this sacred season, may we make room in our hearts and lives for your presence and direction. May these passages open space in us to receive your word in a new way, a way that leads to abundant life. May this Lenten season be a time of repentance, renewal, and reconciliation. Amen.

Ideas for Preaching on Matthew 6:1-6, 16-21

Upon first reading the text found in Matthew, it can sound like a list of what not to do. It almost feels like you're in trouble before you even start. Perhaps this is one of the reasons we tend to enter the Lenten season with dread, especially on Ash Wednesday when we are reminded of our mortality. It can feel like doom and gloom. We are told to "give things up" and" confess our sins." We are told that we come from dust and will return to dust.

While Ash Wednesday can be solemn, it doesn't have to be bleak. What if instead of entering the Lenten season with trepidation and fear, we entered it with gratitude and joy? Lent is an invitation to draw closer to God, ourselves, and one another. Then we can read Matthew's text as a playbook for how to participate in this sacred time with authenticity, vulnerability, and thoughtfulness. It is a summoning of our true selves to return to God. It is a call for us to examine our intentions and motivations. Do we attend church, volunteer, make a big show of giving for the applause of our peers, or do we do these things because we have been transformed by a loving God?

Jesus assumes that followers participate in all three of these spiritual practices: almsgiving, prayer, and fasting. Jesus does not say, "*if* you give, pray, fast"; he says *when*. So, the question becomes *why* do you participate in these disciplines? Is it for other's approval, or is it to draw closer to God?

The real reward is not chasing accolades but rather deep relationship and intimacy with God. If the recognition were to dissipate, would we still do these things?

Bringing the Text to Life

The word *slacktivism* was coined in 1995. "It is the practice of supporting a political or social cause by means such as social media or online petitions, characterized as involving very little effort or commitment."[1] While not all online support should be discounted, if it is not working in conjunction with true commitment to social causes, it can be seen as self-seeking.

There are many motivations for why people behave the way that they do. It is quite possible that we are never fully free of our own egos. However, if our spiritual participation is grounded in our need for praise or recognition, we're missing it. We will get caught up in those distractions and never enter into the fullness that is promised. Lent is a good time to take inventory and to realign our head, heart, and hands.

Ideas for Preaching on Joel 2:1-2, 12-17

The second chapter of Joel picks up after a devastating locust plague and drought in Jerusalem. While scholars cannot pinpoint the exact "sin(s)" of Israel, it is thought that this was the consequence of some human action. Despite the people of Zion feeling secure within the Persian empire, the prophet Joel is reminding them that ultimately God is in control. This is a good reminder for those of us living in the United States of America. Our sense of stability and security is indeed a false one.

Joel is imploring the community to return to the Lord. However, Joel is not asking them to engage in the typical tearing of clothing to outwardly showcase their repentance but rather to rend their hearts as an inward and authentic return to God.

In ancient Israel, the heart was thought of as the seat of the emotional and intellectual life.[2] So, to return to God with all your heart meant complete dedication. It was stopping in the direction that led away from God and turning to walk back toward God. God is continually giving us the opportunity to return; however, it is our decision. We must decide if we will truly repent.

The second blowing of the trumpet is an invitation for all people to gather and repent. None are exempt and all are welcome. God's grace and love are available. How will we respond?

Bringing the Text to Life

One of my favorite words is *metanoia*. Often the translation for *metanoia* is "repentance." However, many scholars agree that this is incorrect.[3]

In Greek the prefix *meta* means "beyond" and the word *noia* is translated to "mind" or "thought." Together a more accurate translation of *metanoia* is to "change your mind." It can also mean to turn in a new direction or go a different way. The prophet Joel is urging Israel to change not only their hearts but their minds and actions as well.

Ash Wednesday is an appropriate time to talk about *metanoia* and to invite people to change their minds. To turn to acknowledge the things that are causing brokenness in their lives and to choose to go a different way.

It is by God's grace that we are invited to—again and again—choose a new direction. We are continually offered opportunities to return to God with our whole hearts. However, we must choose to do so. God's grace demands a response. We are responsible to answer God's call. Preachers might ask their communities, "How might you answer God's call to turn around this Lenten season?"

Notes

March 9, 2025–First Sunday in Lent

Deuteronomy 26:1-11; Psalm 91:1-2, 9-16; **Romans 10:8b-13;**
Luke 4:1-13

Chelsea Simon

Preacher to Preacher Prayer

Loving God, we are tempted by so many things in this world—power, wealth, prestige. Help us to resist the various temptations that seek to distract us from you. Let us find strength in your word and in your spirit. May these readings remind us of your deep love for us and your desire to be in relationship with us.

Ideas for Preaching on Luke 4:1-13

This familiar Lenten text is entitled "The Testing of Jesus." I often wonder why Jesus needed to be tested. Was it to prove to himself that he could handle the pressures of public ministry? Or to demonstrate to others that he was worthy of their devotion? Did he have some inner demons he had to work out? Or was it to teach us, the future readers, about the importance of obedience?

These are all, quite possibly, valid directions the preacher could take with this text. Jesus's time in the wilderness takes place directly following his baptism in the Jordan River. He is "full of the Holy Spirit" (v. 1). Before he begins his public ministry, he makes a pit stop for forty days in the wilderness. During this time, Jesus fasted and was tempted by the devil. The tempter tries to lure Jesus with various worldly pleasures.

Just as we have the power to choose, so did Jesus. Jesus could have, at any point, given in to the temptations. However, he did not. His spirit of devotion, faithfulness, and love allowed him to resist the false desires of the world and remain steadfast in his mission.

Perhaps this time in the wilderness—these forty days (not counting Sundays) of Lent—can provide us a time to put down the worldly distractions of prestige, prosperity, and power and open ourselves to the love, grace, and life of God. As Ronald Rolheiser says, Lent invites us to "open ourselves up to the chaos of the desert so that we can finally give the angels a chance to feed us."[4] How might the angels feed us during this time?

Bringing the Text to Life

- Akiva ben Yosef, a first-century rabbi, was walking home after a late night of studying the Torah. He was captivated by the Hebrew scriptures and was so deep in thought that he lost his way. He suddenly found himself at the gate of a Roman military compound.

- Rabbi Akiva was so disoriented that before he could turn around, a Roman guard shouted down to him, "Who are you? Why are you here?"

  The Rabbi, while still startled and bewildered, could only respond, "What?"

  The guard again asked, "Who are you? Why are you here?"

  The Rabbi smiled and asked, "How much do you get paid to ask those questions?"

  The guard responded, "Two shekels a day."

  Rabbi Akiva then looked up at the guard and said, "I will pay you twice that if you follow me to my home and ask me those very same questions every single morning."

- Irish poet and theologian Pádraig Ó Tuama points out that the word *if* that the devil uses to tempt Jesus is of extreme importance. The Greek word *ei* is equivalent to "since" or "that"; therefore, the challenge isn't about Jesus's identity but rather how he uses his power.[5] How do we use ours? How do we use our agency and free will and responsibility in every moment?

Ideas for Preaching on Romans 10:8b-13

The church in Rome was established by the time they received this letter from Paul; however, they were experiencing great divisions based on the various customs and traditions. Jews and non-Jews disagreed about how to follow Jesus, who was included, food practices, and so on. Paul was writing to this divided community to bring about unity.

To do this Paul reminds the church in Rome that "all have sinned and fall short of God' glory" (Romans 3:23) *and* all are welcomed into salvation through the recognition of Jesus Christ as Lord. Paul says that all can be saved. While the church is fighting about the Jewish versus Gentile ways of following Jesus, Paul says, "there is no distinction between Jew and Greek" (Romans 8:12).

The good news of Jesus is for all people. We share in the same brokenness, and we can share in the same hope. And this hope is not far away; it is near. It is as close to us as our mouth and heart. We do not have to wait for this salvation. It is for us to claim now. We can be transformed by grace *today*. How might this time of Lent lead us to deeper and more meaningful transformation?

Bringing the Text to Life

- The cartoon entitled *Eraser Jesus* reminds us that the lines we draw in the sand are arbitrary. Jesus came to erase the lines, tear down the walls, and get rid of all the things that divide us. Everyone is in.[6]

- Artist, author, and speaker Scott Erickson creates profound and meaningful works of art. The adventurous preacher might show an image of his and lead the congregation in a *Visio Divina* experience. During *Visio Divina*, participants will focus on an image while they invoke prayer, imagination, creativity, and openness, as the sacred appears to them in perhaps a new way. This work of Erickson's is entitled *Trinity Hug.*[7] Recently he posted it on his social media pages with this conversation:

  "Where are You?" I asked.

  "I'm hiding out in every single person you meet. Look for me there."[8]

  All hold the image of God within themselves. This is our gift and irrefutably gives us dignity and worth.

Notes

March 16, 2025–Second Sunday in Lent

Genesis 15:1-12, 17-18; **Psalm 27***; Philippians 3:17-4:1;* **Luke 13:31-35**
or Luke 9:28-36, (37-43a)

Chelsea Simon

Preacher to Preacher Prayer

Mother Hen, thank you for gathering us into you, under your wings, close to your heart. Keep us there and let us feel your comfort, even in the midst of trouble or pain. You are our help, our shield, and our protector. Remind us that you love us and that you will never leave. Teach us to walk in your ways. We trust that they will lead to life and life abundant. Amen.

Ideas for Preaching on Luke 13:31-35

The common adage "the fox in the henhouse" serves as a metaphor referring to a predator who will strike if given the opportunity. This can happen when someone who is less than trustworthy, perhaps even malicious, is given a position of power that allows them to take advantage of the less fortunate for their own personal gain.

When we pick up our reading in the Luke 13, Jesus has begun his march to Jerusalem. The march that will inevitably end in his death. The Pharisees even try to warn Jesus. They say, "Herod is going to kill you. You need to get out of here." I don't know about you, but that would be enough to get me moving along.

However, Jesus is not deterred. He knows he is here for a specific mission and not even death will keep him from it. Jesus basically says, "I will move on when I decide to. I know my death is coming, and I must make it to Jerusalem before that happens."

I imagine Jesus sharing his decision with some force, or at the very least strong conviction. Then he kind of changes his tone. He pulls out this feminine metaphor of a mother hen. This is not the typical image we have of Jesus, and it certainly wouldn't be what the Jewish audience would have wanted or expected to hear. They had expected the Messiah to be someone who would save them from Roman occupation by the only way they knew: force. A powerful warrior who would come and save the day by destroying their enemies.

Jesus just doesn't play by the world's rules. He likens himself to a mother hen who is looking to protect the poor and marginalized from the deception and exploitation of the powerful. Jesus is willing to stand in between the fox and his chicks. There is likely nothing a mother hen can do to actually protect the livelihood of her chicks. She will probably lose her life in the attempt to protect them from harm. But she will be with them in the battle. She will not forsake them or leave them to fend for themselves. This is who we have in Jesus. A presence who will not leave us, no matter how threatening the situation. No matter how real the threat. We have a God who loves us enough to stay in the fight with us.

Bringing the Text to Life

- In artist Kelly Latimore's icon entitled *Christ: The Mother Hen,* we see the image of a protecting and gathering presence, a stoic and strong advocate for the well-being of the vulnerable.[9] Daryl Davis exhibited great courage amid potentially threatening circumstances. Daryl, an African American blues musician, had a chance encounter with a white Ku Klux Klan member following a performance one evening. He began to rethink the animosity between Black and White people and wondered if the hate might be misunderstood. As a result of that meeting Daryl started connecting with KKK members to discuss where the hatred and prejudice originated. Because of their relationship with Daryl, over two hundred people have left the Klan, gifting Daryl with their infamous white robes as they left. Despite the potential risk to his own well-being, Daryl worked to change the trajectory of not only other Black people's lives, but also the lives of those KKK members who were imprisoned by hatred and fear.[10]

- Recent studies have found that mother hens can actually empathize with their chicks. As it turns out, mother hens show visible signs of anxiety when their chicks are in danger. Due to their "attentive, caring parenting they 'feel' their chicks' pain."[11] How much more so than God?

Ideas for Preaching on Psalm 27

I am always amazed at the breadth of emotion and depth of honesty found in the Psalms. They speak to the human experience in all its complexities. The authors do not withhold their heartfelt expressions to God. They trust that God can handle it and they demand that God be faithful to the past promises.

In Psalm 27, the psalmist is afraid and seeking God's comfort and protection. These fears might be real or imagined. Many of our fears live in this uncertain and futuristic place. Our fears could come to fruition or not. Lack of control might play a role in anxieties. The realization that we are finite beings who have limitations can cause some existential stress.

It is in submitting to our humanness and recognition of God's limitlessness that we can find comfort. We can turn over the worries of tomorrow to a God who holds it all.

Bringing the Text to Life

- The serenity prayer is a helpful resource when talking about control, power, comfort, agency, and submissiveness. Traditionally attributed to theologian Reinhold Niebuhr, the prayer has become an Alcoholic Anonymous staple. It is typically described in a threefold request for serenity, courage, and wisdom. Couldn't we all use more of all three?

- John Wesley's Covenant Prayer might also be a helpful farming for this psalm. It talks about submitting one's life to the will of God, trusting in God's provision, love, and graciousness.[12]

Notes

March 23, 2025–Third Sunday in Lent

Isaiah 55:1-9; **Psalm 63:1-8**; 1 Corinthians 10:1-13; **Luke 13:1-9**

Chelsea Simon

Preacher to Preacher Prayer

Dear God, at times we need to take care of others, and at times we need to be taken care of. Remind us of the reciprocal nature of community and connection. Give us courage to recognize and ask for what we need. Grant us the strength to care for others, even when they are not "performing" how we want or expect them to. Amen.

Ideas for Preaching on Luke 13:1-9

The story of the fruitless fig tree would have been familiar to Jesus's listeners. It echoes back to the Old Testament's telling of another barren garden (Isaiah 5:1-7). However, in the Isaiah story the plants are not given grace or time. The garden is destroyed. So, in Jesus's retelling of it, the radicalness of patience would have been realized. After three years, surely this fig tree should be producing fruit, and yet it is not. The owner says, "Let's cut our losses and move on." The gardener proposes not only another year but also additional care (i.e., more manure).

At times, I act as the tree owner. I believe people should be further along, more together, at a different place. When they are not, I want to write them off. I put my preconceived notions and expectations onto them and then feel disappointed when they don't perform how I believe they should perform.

Other times (although far less frequent), I am the gardener. I can offer grace, understanding, and special attention. Somehow a place of compassion will open in me, and I have space to allow people to be themselves, however imperfect.

And still other times, I am the barren tree. I am in need of time, space, and attentiveness. I am unable to produce or achieve. In these humbling moments, I count on the empathy of others to offer me what I need.

Bringing the Text to Life

What would it look like to tell this parable from the perspective of all three main characters (owner, gardener, and tree)? Perhaps providing the different perspectives could give people permission to recognize the different places they might find themselves.

One might even invite others to participate in sharing or reading a perspective. Costumes also might help hold the congregation's interest. This is a great way to remind the community that everyone sees the world through different lenses.

Ideas for Preaching on Psalm 63:1-8

What a beautiful poem of devotion and love, often attributed to David. The psalmist is speaking not only of God's ultimacy but also of his intimacy with God. God's majesty and might do not stand as a barrier to relationship but rather as an invitation to come close. There is a trust in the steadfast love, protection, and connection with God that allows him to honestly share the innermost parts of his heart.

David is in the Judean wilderness, a barren place wherein thirst and hunger are real bodily needs. And yet, he is reaching out to the Giver of Life to meet his needs in a way that is perhaps deeper than just meeting his physical needs. Here he is expressing a profound longing of the human heart.

What is perhaps most interesting about this passage is *where* the psalmist is doing the praising. It is not in the presence of a priest or within the walls of a temple. It is in his own bed (v. 6). The ever-persistent thirst and hunger for God does not only emerge on Sundays between 11:00 a.m. and 12:00 p.m., but all of the time. David trusts that God is present and hears him. God is available whenever and wherever we are.

We know that God does not exist only within our sanctuaries or places of worship. But do we know that in our hearts? In our souls? In our overextended schedules? How might we carry this desire and devotion for God into all aspects of our lives?

Bringing the Text to Life

Brother Lawrence (born Nicolas Herman) was a lay brother in a Carmelite monastery during the 1600s. As a teenager, Nicolas had a spiritual experience while serving in the army. One day, in the middle of the battleground, he saw a barren tree and had an epiphany. In just three months' time that tree would be full of leaves and flowers. It would come back to life. He saw this tree as a metaphor for God's desire and ability for transformation (hint, hint: fig tree).

After his time in the army, Nicolas sought a religious life in the Order of Discalced Carmelites (OCD), where he took on the name Brother Lawrence. His job at the monastery was to serve in the kitchen. Despite his humble position, people were drawn to him for his wisdom and ability to cultivate deep connection with God. His spiritual guidance, found in both letters and in conversations, became the foundation of the well-known book *The Practice of the Presence of God.*

Brother Lawrence did not separate the world into secular and sacred time; rather he intentionally sought God's presence in even the most mundane of tasks, such as washing the dishes. Lawrence once said, the time of business is not different from the time of prayer; in the noise of my kitchen, I feel I am on my knees at the blessed sacrament.[13] How might we emulate the psalmist and Brother Lawrence by finding God in all the places and people that make up our world? Sometimes we can view the world as a distraction from God. We can get so preoccupied with tasks that we forget about God. But what if we could shift our thinking to bring God into those tasks, no matter how mundane? We have to remember that God is not absent, not ever. It is only our awareness of God that is absent. Let us cultivate that during this Lenten season.

Notes

March 30, 2025–Fourth Sunday in Lent

Joshua 5:9-12; Psalm 32; **2 Corinthians 5:16-21; Luke 15:1-3, 11b-32**

Chelsea Simon

Preacher to Preacher Prayer

Patient and expecting God, you never give up on us. You keep watching, waiting for our hearts to return. When they do, you open your arms wide and welcome us home. Give us the courage to admit when we are lost and the strength to turn back home. May we hear this familiar story in a new way as we prepare for this week's worship. Amen.

Ideas for Preaching on Luke 15:1-3, 11b-32

The story of the prodigal son is among Jesus's most memorable and well-loved stories. Even non-church goers might be able to tell you the gist of this parable. Because it is so well known, we can often gloss over it, assuming we know what it has to teach us.

Typically, the focus is on the extravagant love of the father, the glorious welcome home, and the fattened calf at the party. However, a lot happens leading up to this celebration. The son prematurely takes his father's inheritance, which was taboo since his father was still living. The son takes his new money and goes off to explore the world. I am sure he had a great time, but before long he ran out of money and a famine hit. Times get tough and the younger son is left with two options: continue to live with pigs while starving or admit to himself (and then his father) that he made a mistake.

Pride can be an extremely difficult thing to overcome. I can think of many people who would rather suffer than admit they were wrong, even though admitting wrongdoing could bring about peace, joy, and fullness of life.

The son, who is often demonized as selfish and disrespectful, models for us what it means to confront our mistakes and seek reconciliation. He did not know how his father would receive him. He was unaware of the grace that was waiting for him. He expected to work as a servant for his father and he was ready to face those consequences.

I wonder how many of us have allowed guilt and shame to keep us from God's grace. How many of us have continued to sit in our own suffering instead of reconciling with the God of love? God does not leave us because we make mistakes, but often we allow our mistakes to keep us from God. We get consumed by our shame and think, "God can't forgive that." What would happen if we could trust in God's unending, unconditional, and all-encompassing love?

Bringing the Text to Life

Brené Brown talks about the difference between guilt and shame. She says, "guilt says, 'I did something bad,' whereas shame says, 'I am bad.'"[14] GoD and DoG is a sweet video/story/song about the unconditional love of God. While the lyrics are simplistic in nature, they speak deep spiritual truths about God's patient and expectant nature. Both God and dog await our return and celebrate when we come home.[15] Following apartheid in South Africa, President Nelson Mandela established the Truth and Reconciliation Commission and appointed Archbishop Desmond Tutu as the chairperson. The goal of this commission was to provide perpetrators of violence to share their stories and request amnesty. The commission focused on reconciliation and restorative justice as opposed to retributive justice. This countercultural way of responding to violence allowed for victims and assailants to find peace and forgiveness.

Ideas for Preaching on 2 Corinthians 5:16-21

Paul writes this letter to the church in Corinth after he learns of some division over certain practices and traditions. He encourages them to remain united despite their disagreements. The goal of this letter is to reconcile the community and recenter them on the primary mission of following Jesus.

In this particular passage, Paul is insisting that everyone has value and worth because of Christ. We are new creations through Christ and our past transgressions are not held against us. Therefore, others' value, dignity, and worthiness does not depend on how they behave or our expectations of them. Paul is saying they have intrinsic and unconditional worth because of Christ, regardless of their actions.

As followers of Christ, we must not be distracted by self-centered notions such as who is worthy of love, who is considered valuable, who deserves dignity and respect. Our requirements mean nothing because "old things have gone away, and look, new things have arrived" (v. 17).

Any good therapist might tell you that the faults you find in others may very well be the aspects of yourself that you find less than desirable. We tend to demonize others for the exact behavior or motivations that drive ourselves. Shame and self-loathing can find sneaky ways of coming to the surface. Those things we thought we had buried deep inside, those attributes we thought no one would know about, those past mistakes we tried to forget.

However, acceptance, respect, and understanding are the very things others need to feel safe enough to be themselves. When everyone is in and no one is out, the

Beloved Community begins to take shape. The love of God is felt in the lives of others and in our own lives.

Bringing the Text to Life

In 1995, college student Tariq Khamisa was out delivering pizzas when he was shot and killed as part of a gang initiation. Fourteen-year-old Tony Hicks was convicted as an adult and sentenced to twenty-five years to life in prison. Tariq's father, Azim Khamisa, saw both boys as victims and promptly forgave Tony.

To begin the process of reconciliation, Azim contacted Tony's grandfather, Ples Felix. Azim recognized that both he and Ples were grieving and in need of healing. Together, Azim and Ples started The Tariq Khamisa Foundation (TKF). Their mission is to "create safer schools and communities through educating and inspiring children in the restorative principles of accountability, compassion, forgiveness, and peacemaking."[16] Five years after the murder, Azim visited Tony in prison and the two stayed in touch. In 2019 Tony was released from prison. He now spends time volunteering for the foundation.

This heartbreaking situation could have paralyzed and ruined many lives, but Azim saw Tony not as a human would see him but as Christ sees him. He was able to offer forgiveness and to work toward reconciliation and in the process heal himself, Ples, Tony, and many more.

Notes

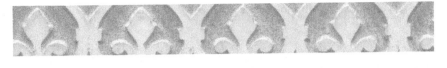

April 6, 2025–Fifth Sunday in Lent

Isaiah 43:16-21; *Psalm 126*; *Philippians 3:4b-14*; *John 12:1-8*

Jennifer Wyant

Preacher to Preacher Prayer

Loving God, we know that you are always our Creator God. We read that you are making all things new. You are always our redeeming God. You restore even the most broken parts of ourselves and our world. Help us to bear witness to the work you are always doing in our midst, so that we might point people to you in all things. Amen.

Ideas for Preaching on Isaiah 43:16-21

This passage in Isaiah is a powerful testimony to God's faithfulness and creativity, written to a people who had recently lost everything. They had been sent into exile and found themselves living in a foreign land, surrounded by enemies, and it is against this backdrop that they are told that God was going to make a way out of no way. God says, "I'm doing a new thing; now it sprouts up; don't you recognize it? I'm making a way in the desert, paths in the wilderness" (v. 19).

The author reminds his audience that they serve a God who once cut a path through the middle of the sea and destroyed an entire underneath the waves. This is a clear reference to Exodus 14, when the people of Israel faced a similarly dire situation and the Pharoah sent the Egyptian army to bring them back after their departure and they found themselves backed up to the Red Sea. When all hope was lost in that moment, God literally parted the sea and saved his people. That same God, Isaiah writes, is the one who will surely make a way again.

For the modern church, this can be used to show how it is exactly God's faithfulness in the past that points us to the fact that God will work in our present and our future to bring us out of our own wilderness and exiles. We serve a God who is always able to do a new thing in our midst if we would just have eyes to see it.

Bringing the Text to Life

- In your context, where have you been seeing God do a new thing? Identify them for your congregation and call them out specifically. This could be a new Sunday school, baptisms, new missions, and so on. God does not only do new things for exiled people in Israel. This text is a great opportunity to highlight the ways you have seen God moving in your context and to speak them out loud to your people.

- There is a fairly popular song by Don Moen called "God Will Make a Way" (1992). He shares the story of its composition and how it was inspired by this passage during a tragic time in his family. You can watch him share that story on YouTube (https://www.youtube.com/watch?v=zwF4grwlPhw).

Ideas for Preaching John 12:1-8

All four Gospels recount a woman washing Jesus's feet with expensive perfume, but John's account is the only one that names the woman as Mary of Bethany and the complaining disciple as Judas Iscariot. This creates a unique dynamic in this version of the story between a character John clearly views as a true follower, Mary of Bethany, and someone John views as a duplicitous follower, Judas Iscariot. In Luke's account, his unnamed woman is described as sinful, and sometimes this can lead to some blending of the accounts, as if John, too, intends us to read Mary as sinful. Be careful when preaching not to make this mistake. You are missing the point of John's story if you blend it with Luke's account.

John is creating this contrast between a true disciple and a fake one. Mary's act of anointing Jesus is lifted up as a pure and holy act of devotion done completely out of love for Jesus. Judas, however, casts aspersions on her act, trying to argue that the better act would have been to take care of the poor with the resources she had. He is trying to "one-up" her perceived goodness and diminish her in the process. John tells us that he is not even sincere in his complaint. He does not actually care about the poor. He wants the money. We are even told that he has been skimming off the top of Jesus's funds. There is no reason to take his complaint in good faith.

There is a tendency among Christians to be judgmental of the works of others. To look at their attempts and show how they were flawed or how they did not pursue the greatest good. But John's account tells us that is the act of a false disciple. Very rarely does a critique of someone else's service come genuinely from a place of Christian affection. Usually, it comes from a desire to put someone down. Especially as we walk toward the end of the Lenten season, this passage is a needed reminder for us to perform our own acts of devotion and extravagant love and to not judge or criticize the acts of others.

Bringing the Text to Life

- You could talk about nard, which is what Mary uses to anoint Jesus. It was one of the most expensive perfumes in the ancient world. It was made from the spike nard plant (from the same family as the modern honeysuckle plant), and its flowers were crushed to make an amber-colored oil-like substance. It has an earthy and sweet smell. Pure nard today can still be pretty expensive, but you can buy cheaper versions of it on Amazon and from other online retailers. It would be a creative way to connect your audience to this story if they could physically smell the nard.

- What Mary does is an act of extravagant love for Jesus, one that seems so over the top in terms of expense, it might be understandable to question it. But what would it look for our congregations to love Jesus extravagantly? We often talk (rightly) about God's extravagant love for us, but in this instance, what would it look like for you to challenge your congregation to practice extravagant love for God?

Notes

April 13, 2025–Palm/Passion Sunday

Psalm 118:1-2, 19-29; Luke 19:28-40; Isaiah 50:4-9a;
Psalm 31:9-16; Philippians 2:5-11; *Luke 22:14-23:56*

Jennifer Wyant

Preacher to Preacher Prayer

God of both our good days and our bad days, we know you are with us when we celebrate and when we mourn. Either way, we rejoice in this day you have made. Help us find words to remember this last week of your son's life here on earth. Help us find ways to lift up both the joy and the suffering, knowing that in all things, we give thanks. Amen.

A Note on Preaching on Both Palm and Passion

Traditionally, this is the day we celebrate Jesus's triumphal entry into Jerusalem and the official kickoff of Holy Week. But with fewer people able or willing to attend the midweek services of Maundy Thursday and Good Friday, it is important to help people also look toward the cross in this service, or else they might go from the celebration of Palm Sunday to the celebration of Easter without reflecting on the death of Jesus. Because of this, many pastors choose to focus on Jesus's passion either instead or in conjunction with the triumphal entry. While attempting two themes in one day is challenging, it can be done well with some planning.

One way that you can accomplish both is through the structure of your service; it doesn't have to rest entirely on the sermon itself to do this. You could begin the service with high energy, a palm procession, a celebratory opening hymn, the reading of the triumphal entry scripture, and so on. As you move through your service, you could bring down the energy, moving into a more contemplative space with a more reflective anthem and a sermon that helps move your congregation toward the cross. Instead of a congregational closing hymn, you could even choose a soloist to sing a more somber piece about Jesus's death and then invite the congregation to depart in silence. Alternatively, you could also start the service with a Palm Sunday Gospel reading and then end the service with a reading of the crucifixion scene.

Ideas for Preaching on Psalm 118:1-2, 19-29

While this text isn't the standard Palm Sunday reading, it is one of the scriptures referenced by Matthew shortly after Jesus's entry into the city, and more broadly it is a psalm of praise that fits the overall themes of this day perfectly. On one hand, this psalm emphasizes God's victory and God's goodness. "Give thanks to the LORD," the psalmist writes, "because he is good, because his steadfast love lasts forever" (v. 29). God is going to act and save the righteous and all will be well. It is a celebration that matches the tone of Jesus's entry into Jerusalem when the people shout praises and lay down palms.

But on the other hand, there are moments in this psalm that can be used to allude to what is coming. The psalmist mentions the stone that is rejected (v. 22), and earlier in the psalm, he repeatedly mentions his distress and how he turned to cry out to the Lord for salvation. The Lord does save, and thus, there is praise and thanksgiving. But it doesn't mean there wasn't a cost. It also doesn't mean that everything was easy.

On the one hand, you could use this psalm to highlight the triumph and the joy of Jesus's entry into Jerusalem and you could highlight how Jesus is later seen as the stone, once rejected, who becomes the cornerstone for salvation. On the other hand, you could make a turn to show that the promise of God's salvation doesn't mean there won't be suffering, and in fact, in the case of holy week, we will see that suffering, specifically Jesus's suffering, becomes central to God's redeeming work in the world, making Palm Sunday a costly celebration.

Bringing the Text to Life

You could discuss cornerstones and their functions in ancient buildings. These were the first stones to be set in any structure, thus making them the principal stones, and all the other stones would be placed using the cornerstones as a reference. Oftentimes, the cornerstone would be a site of ceremonial significance as well. In the first-century church, as a result this reference and its connection to Jesus, cornerstones take on a religious significance as well (Ephesians 2:20 also explicitly labels Jesus as the cornerstone). Because of this, many churches specifically mark their cornerstone with scripture, relics, or artwork. Your church even might have a cornerstone.

Ideas for Preaching on Luke 19:28-40

Luke's account of Jesus's entrance into Jerusalem is very similar to both Mark and Matthew's accounts except for two things. First, Luke omits that the people laid down branches along the road, only mentioning the people's cloaks. Second, it is only in Luke's account where we read the Pharisees attempted to get the people to stop their praising (v. 39), to which Jesus responds famously, "I tell you, if they were silent, the stones would shout" (v. 40). This could potentially be a reference to Habakkuk 2:11, which states: "A stone will cry out from a village wall, and a tree branch will respond." Contextually, Habakkuk is discussing how the stones will speak out the truth and so judgment will come on the evildoers. So, some biblical scholars debate the reference, but the idea that the stones will tell the truth no matter what does connect to the scene at hand. The truth about who Jesus is cannot be contained. The religious leaders are going to try to stop it. They are orchestrating a plot that will end in his death, but even then, they cannot stop it. The good news of Jesus Christ is stronger than them, stronger even than death. Thus, the crowds cry out about the king who comes in the name of the Lord.

Bringing the Text to Life

There is a famous painting that depicts the scene of Jesus looking over Jerusalem after his triumphal entry called the *Flevit super illam* by Enrique Simonet Lombardo. In this painting, which means "he wept over," Jesus is mourning what is to come, not for himself but to the city itself. This painting could be discussed as a turning point from the celebration of the palms to the grief of the passion as it's a beautiful piece that captures the intensity of the moment.

Ideas for Preaching on Luke 22:14–23:56

This very long passage is Luke's account of the Last Supper and arrest, trial, and crucifixion of Jesus Christ. Ideally, you would read through the passage in order to focus on a specific section of the text. I would recommend if you are doing a Palm/ Passion theme, to focus more on the end of Luke 23. In Luke 23:27, there is an echo back to the people crying out to praise God when Jesus enters the city in Luke 19:37, except this time it is a crowd of people and the women are loudly weeping as Jesus exits the city to be crucified. What started as rejoicing ends with weeping. Their hero king is going to his death. And he does die and the sun's light fails, as they watch from a distance. We are told most of the crowd witness what happened and then they go away "beating their breasts" in sadness. But the women stay and watch. They watch when Joseph of Arimathea takes Jesus and wraps him in cloth and places him in the tomb. The story seems over. The king who came in the name of the Lord is dead. They had hoped that he would be the one to save Israel, but it's over. No more rejoicing. The story ends with silence.

Except. Luke has one more chapter left.

Bringing the Text to Life

- Luke's account describes Simon the Cyrene, who is made to carry Jesus's cross. It is a small detail but you could invite your congregation to place themselves in the narrative and imagine what it would be like to carry Jesus's cross in that moment. We are not told anything else about him, and we are not told if he says anything, making it a powerful moment for us to enter the text and see ourselves there.

- Luke also describes Joseph of Arimathea and his retrieval of Jesus's body and placing it in new, rock-hewn tomb. You could share a little about Jewish burial practices from this time period, which typically included placing the deceased in the front of the tomb on a carved-out rock bed for about a year. After this, the body, now bones, would be moved further back into the tomb with the previously deceased ancestors. This is unique because we are explicitly told it's a new tomb, meaning Jesus is the only one there, which would have been fairly rare. Joseph of Arimathea in many ways shows some of the greatest love for Jesus in the whole Gospel narrative. He loves and serves Jesus even when he believes Jesus can't do anything for him in return.

Notes

April 17, 2025–Maundy Thursday

Exodus 12:1-4, (5-10), 11-14; Psalm 116:1-2, 12-19; **1 Corinthians 11:23-26; John 13:1-17, 31b-35**

Jennifer Wyant

Preacher to Preacher Prayer

God of our salvation, help us to hear the story of this night again. Let us not rush past into the pain of tomorrow and the victory of Sunday. Help us to sit alongside you with the bread and the wine. Help us to hear your words to love one another. And help us, Jesus, so that we might actually be able to do it. Amen.

Ideas for Preaching on 1 Corinthians 11:23-26

This passage on holy Communion in Paul's first letter to the Corinthians is brief but is one of the few times Paul gives us insight into what he was taught about Jesus's earthly life. Paul often focuses on the death and resurrection of Jesus and the implications of the risen Lord, but here he offers to us the earliest account of Communion as he recites what Jesus did on the night before he was handed over to be killed. (Remember, even though this letter comes after the Gospels, Paul wrote it a few decades before Luke wrote his account).

Within the context of 1 Corinthians 11, Paul is actually condemning how the Corinthians have been practicing the Lord's Supper. He accuses them of letting their poorer brothers and sisters go hungry at the Lord's table while others feast. He accuses them of having divisions even at the Lord's table and says this is counter to everything Jesus intended. This is a powerful charge to us still today. How are we allowing our divisions to cause harm? In separating ourselves are we doing harm to our neighbor? Christ died, offered his body and his blood, and in doing so, brought us together as one people, one body, one church. Let us not divide what God has brought together, especially at the Lord's table.

Bringing the Text to Life

- You could highlight how the words Paul recites about the Last Supper in early 50s CE and the words we say almost two thousand years later when we take Communion are so similar. Generations upon generations of Christians have been telling this same story about Jesus's actions on this last night. And on this Maundy Thursday we join in the chorus of believers through the centuries. We continue to do this in remembrance of him. This could be a good transition moment into Communion.

- In the tenth and eleventh centuries, there was a huge fight in the church about bread. Specifically, Communion bread and whether or not it should be leavened or unleavened. This fight got so heated that eventually the leader of the Catholic Church and the leader of the Orthodox Church excommunicated each other in 1054, in what we know as the Great Papal Schism. This is a great story to tie into how Christians are and have been constantly fighting to divide ourselves even over things like the shape of bread. We come by it honestly, but Christ calls us to unity, calls us to love one another, like he loved us.

Ideas for Preaching on John 13:1-17, 31b-35

John's Gospel doesn't feature Jesus instituting the Lord's Supper during his last meal with his disciples like the other Gospels. Instead, John features something unique among the Gospel narratives of this last night with his disciples: Jesus washing his disciples' feet. John's description of this act is vivid and detailed, describing the specifics of each step of this act of devotion. The whole story is set against the backdrop that Jesus knows this is his last night with them. We are told in verse 1 that "having loved his own who were in the world, he loved them fully."

John then inserts an interesting small detail, a mention of Judas Iscariot and the fact that the devil had already decided that Judas would betray Jesus. Here and again in verse 26, we are made aware of Judas and his presence at this last gathering. John is reminding us that Jesus still permits Judas to be present here despite Jesus knowing what will happen. Jesus still washes Judas's feet.

In doing so, John shows us that Jesus doesn't just serve those who are faithful to him; he even serves his enemy. He serves those who will forsake him in a few short hours. And he insists that they should go and do likewise, go and serve one another.

Bringing the Text to Life

- Traditionally, in the Roman Catholic Church, the pope will wash the feet of twelve high-ranking priests on Maundy Thursday. However, on Pope Francis's first Maundy Thursday, he decided to wash the feet of people in prison, including those of two women, in the rite. Pope Francis said he did this because he wanted to be closer to those who were suffering during holy week. Despite the immense amount of pushback, he still does this practice every year.[1] Maundy Thursday comes from the Latin *mandatum*, which means "commandment." This is for the new commandment in John 13 that Jesus gives the disciples: that they love one another like he has loved them.

- Foot-washing as a spiritual practice can be a powerful part of a Maundy Thursday service. You can, of course, talk about the traditions around foot-washing in the life of the church. Some churches include this every year as part of their traditional holy week services; but for many congregations, it can be unfamiliar and perhaps uncomfortable. An alternative suggestion as a way to include this practice, as opposed to having it during the literal service, is to provide a space after the service where people can choose to go and participate. You could also include it with other prayer stations, inviting people into a contemplative time after the conclusion of the Maundy Thursday service.

Notes

April 18, 2025–Good Friday

*Isaiah 52:13-53:12; **Psalm 22**; Hebrews 10:16-25 or*
*Hebrews 4:14-16, 5:7-9; **John 18:1-19:42***

Jennifer Wyant

Preacher to Preacher Prayer

God, in even our darkest moments, we search for you. Like the psalmist, we too cry out to you. Please do not be far away. Help us to find you in the midst of suffering. As we remember your suffering on the cross, help us hold fast to the love we find there still and help us offer it to others.

Ideas for Preaching on Psalm 22

Psalm 22 is an intense lament psalm in its own right, a vivid and desperate plea, begging God to save the psalmist from his imminent death. But it is made even more poignant by the fact that Jesus quotes Psalm 22:1 on the cross in both Mark's and Matthew's account of Jesus's crucifixion. "My God! My God, why have you left me all alone?" Jesus says while hanging on the cross. It is one of the most devastating moments in the entire New Testament. And yet, when Jesus quotes the first line, he is in a way invoking the entire psalm, which starts with lament over the psalmist's perceived abandonment but ends with a turn toward faith, with the belief that God did not turn his face away from him when he called out (v. 24).

On Good Friday, as the preacher you are always balancing the message of the crucifixion with the good news of Easter morning. It is a moment of despair, but it is not the last moment of Jesus's story. Psalm 22 is a great way to hold that balance. The psalmist is expressing pure despair. "I'm poured out like water. All my bones have fallen apart. . . . You've set me down in the dirt of death," he writes (vv. 14-15). He is surrounded by his enemies and they are casting lots for his clothes (22:18, another parallel to Jesus's crucifixion). There is no one to help him, only those who would destroy him. And yet, the psalmist holds to the belief that God "didn't despise or detest the suffering of the one who suffered" (v. 24). The psalmist believes, even in his current moment of suffering, even though all hope is lost, that God will restore him and that one day people will tell the tale of his deliverance. What a powerful message to bring to those who are currently suffering, for those who are without hope, that one, even Jesus felt that way once, and two, that our God is a God who does not forsake us, who can save and does save us, even when all seems lost.

Bringing the Text to Life

- This is a powerful psalm that often doesn't get read in its entirety. Often, only the portions that are referenced at the crucifixion get discussed. But the whole thing is so fitting for Good Friday. Getting a good reader from your congregation or a group of people to read this passage can be really impactful, especially if read at the close of your message. Alternatively, there is a dramatic reading video if that would work better for your context.[2]

- If you are focusing on only the words of Jesus from the cross, you could mention that Luke and John both exclude this saying of Jesus in their accounts. This could be a good jumping off point to think about why. What is so intense about Psalm 22:1 that John and Luke feel more comfortable going with other sayings of Jesus from the cross?

Ideas for Preaching on John 18:1-19:42

This is an extremely long lectionary text, spanning two full chapters. My number one recommendation for preaching on this passage is to read through a time or two and choose a single part to focus on for your sermon. If you try to cover the whole thing in its entirety, it will be too much. You can, of course, tell the whole story to remind your congregation of the details surrounding Jesus's death in John, but you should narrow down to a specific subset for the primary focus on your sermon. Here are a few recommendations of where you could focus a Good Friday sermon:

- You could focus on Pilate's sign that he places over Jesus's cross: "The King of the Jews." In John's account, the religious leaders get mad at this and want the sign to read instead that Jesus claims to be the King of the Jews. Pilate doesn't back down and the sign stands. In John, there is a focus on the truth, and here we see that even though Jesus's enemies want to deny this, the truth of who Jesus is still stands.

- Another place you could focus could be Jesus's conversation with the beloved disciple at the cross where Jesus entrusts him with the care of his mother, who is also said to be present at the cross. It is a powerful scene of Jesus's ongoing love and affection for this mother.

- You could also focus on the extended scene where Jesus's legs are not broken, which connects to Psalm 22:18. In John's account, Jesus is stabbed in the side and blood and water pour out of the wound. In the early church, this became a sign of the sacraments: the blood of the Eucharist and the waters of baptisms, both represented in this moment immediately following Jesus's death.

Bringing this Text to Life

- If you are focusing on Jesus's interaction with his mother, you could show and discuss the *Pieta* by Michelangelo (1499), which is a sculpture depicting Mary holding the recently deceased Jesus in her arms after his crucifixion. It is a striking and powerful image that fully brings to life the grief of Jesus's death. It currently resides in the Basilica of St. Peter in the Vatican.

- If you are focusing on the blood and water coming out of Jesus's side, John Chrysostom preached an amazing sermon on this passage in the fifth century. He preached that this moment when blood and water both came out, it was the moment the church began, as the water represents our baptism and the blood represents the Eucharist. Even though it's a mystery, he argues that when we come to Jesus's side, we too are brought into the church and the family of God.[3]

Easter Vigil

The Easter Vigil is a service that typically happens on Holy Saturday, the day we remember Jesus in the tomb and await his coming resurrection. It is perhaps less commonly practiced than Maundy Thursday or Good Friday in the modern era, but it was traditionally one of the most important services of the Christian year, usually beginning late at night on Holy Saturday and ending after midnight, ushering in the Easter season. The service is a series of liturgy, prayers, scriptures, and the sacraments. It is a remembrance of the Passover of Christ, celebrating when Jesus passed from death to life. Through its many scripture readings, it rehearses the biblical narrative beginning with creation and moving through God's covenant with Abraham, the exodus, the prophets, and then finally moving to a reading of the resurrection of Jesus Christ. It places the celebration of the resurrection within the larger context of God's work in the world. It also includes baptism and communion. (If there is no one needing to be baptized, a service to remember your baptism is appropriate). Within the early church, new Christians were always baptized and initiated into God's church at the Easter Vigil. It is a beautiful and ancient way to await the resurrection of Jesus. Think of it as the parallel to Christmas Eve, only an Easter Eve. It rarely includes a sermon, but words of encouragement or a short homily would be appropriate, and it always ends with the proclamation of the good news that Jesus Christ is risen indeed.

Notes

April 20, 2025–Easter Sunday

Isaiah 65:17-25; Psalm 118:1-2, 14-24; **1 Corinthians 15:19-26;**
Luke 24:1-12

Jennifer Wyant

Preacher to Preacher Prayer

God of all praise and honor glory, we have come to the tomb once more and find it empty. We proclaim the good news of your resurrection: that the last enemy to be defeated is death. That not even death can separate us from your love. That Jesus Christ is risen indeed. Help us to find the words to share this good news with the world. Amen.

Ideas for Preaching on 1 Corinthians 15:19-26

First Corinthians 15 is one of the most important chapters in the New Testament on the nature and importance of the resurrection, but it can be a little complicated to unpack. That said, it is a powerful Easter text because Paul is sharing with the Corinthian congregation why the resurrection matters more than anything else that has ever happened in the world. In chapter 15, he's both sharing the story of the resurrection and who Jesus appeared to after he rose from the dead but also correcting some misconceptions about it. He argues that if Jesus did not raise from the dead then all our faith is in vain. Your faith is futile, he literally says, and we should all be pitied.

But Jesus did rise, and in doing so, Jesus defeated death. He argues that like Adam, who brought death into the world, Jesus did the opposite. He removed the stain of our sins and defeated death through his resurrection. Paul says you can't remove this part of our belief system; the whole thing hinges on it. Without it, Jesus was a good man in a line of good men killed by bad people. The enemies of sin and death had an ironclad grasp over humanity, but then Jesus walked out of that tomb. The good news, according to Paul, is not just that God sent Jesus but that Jesus died and rose again. And that it really happened and that people witnessed it. The resurrection is not an abstract theological concept but a bodily, historical one. God saved the world and the last enemy to be defeated was death. Alleluia!

Bringing the Text to Life

- I know I just discussed a Chrysostom sermon for Good Friday, but he also has an Easter sermon in which he describes death as a monster, a dragon, that plagues everyone and thought it had swallowed Jesus whole. But the good news of Easter, according to Chrysostom, is that Jesus burst through the dragon, cut his way back out, and doing so slayed the dragon for all of us. Jesus, the dragon slayer of death, is a great image for the resurrection.

- One thing to make Paul's writing a little more relatable is that you could discuss all the people that Paul mentions witness the risen Lord. At one point, he says Jesus appeared to five hundred people. Help your congregation put themselves in the shoes of those people who actually saw Jesus—the people whose names aren't recorded in scripture. What was it like for them? How did they respond?

Ideas for Preaching on Luke 24:1-12

Luke's account of the women at the empty tomb is similar to Mark's and Matthew's in many ways. The women go to the tomb to find it empty and to find two men in dazzling clothes who offer a message to them: He is not here. He is risen. Luke tells us that the women remember Jesus's words and how he had told them about this and so they run back to tell the disciples. They are the first ones to proclaim this very best news. But Luke says that when they get there and relay the message that they are not believed. Luke says that their "words struck the apostles as nonsense" (v. 11). The very first sermon of sorts was thought to be nonsense. And maybe that is relatable to all of us preachers.

On a purely literary level, this response makes sense. They are saying the Jesus who they all saw die was not, in fact, dead. This goes against everything the disciples knew to be true about the world. Dead people don't stop being dead. Even people you love. And so, of course, they don't believe. It is easier to find a different explanation, like the women are simply hysterical in their grief.

But on another level, I think the reaction of the disciples strikes at the very heart of the resurrection: it seems too good to be true. The good news is hard to believe. It is hard to actually let yourself receive the message that despite all the suffering, death, and darkness, that God still wins. That God is more powerful than even death. We don't always know if we can believe it: this core truth that in the end, it is all going to work out. That God did not and has not and will never abandon. That no matter how dark it is, the morning is coming. The tomb will be empty. Amen.

Bringing the Text to Life

- Focusing on this idea of news that feels too good to be true, you could share an illustration about Marco Polo, the explorer who traveled along the Silk Road all the way to China in the thirteenth century. He wrote a book about his travels that described all the marvelous and beautiful things he encountered. He was not believed by many as it seemed too good to be true, but he doubled down, saying: "I have not told half of what I saw."

- Another direction would be to focus on how in Luke 24, the women remember that Jesus told them that this was going to happen. You could share how often children have anxiety about parents leaving them at daycare or school and how child psychologists recommend that parents frequently remind their children they will always come back (there's a Daniel Tiger song called "Grown-ups Come Back"). And yet, my son always seems so surprised when I show up at the door. To me, Jesus's resurrection feels a little like that.

Notes

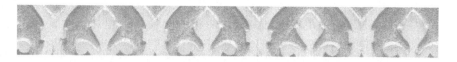

April 27, 2025–Second Sunday of Easter

Acts 5:27-32; Psalm 118:14-29 or **Psalm 150**; *Revelation 1:4-8;* **John 20:19-31**

Chris Jones

Preacher to Preacher Prayer

Lord God, thank you for creating us for worship and meeting us in our doubt. Help us to faithfully follow you with all of who we are. In the name of Jesus, we pray. Amen.

Ideas for Preaching on Psalm 150

The Sunday after Easter is sometimes referred to as "Low Sunday." For preachers, it's a little jarring. Just a week earlier, we put out extra chairs and welcomed more worshippers than normal. Now we're disappointed that our church isn't nearly as full. Thank God for Psalm 150! The psalm reorients us and directs our attention to God, who even after the thrill of that previous Sunday (full congregation or not) continues to be worthy of worship and praise.

We humans are an interesting bunch. We adore attention and prefer to make things about us (a reality that our consumer-driven culture exacerbates). If we're honest, we even make the worship of God about us, from the time and style of service to the music selection and preaching. That's why Psalm 150's tenfold use of "Praise God" and threefold use of "Praise the Lord" is so important. It's the Lord God, not us, who deserves praise. As my seminary professor Richard Hays would remind our class, "It's about God, stupid."

God doesn't just deserve our praise on a single Sunday. God deserves our praise all the time and in every place. Indeed, we humans, along with the rest of creation, were made to "praise the Lord!" (v. 6).

Bringing the Text to Life

- Bishop Dick Wills recalls an incident in which a member of the congregation left because of a shift in music style during the 9:30 a.m. service. Wills proposed that the man attend a different service with music he preferred, but he declined, citing a prior commitment to a tee time at noon. Wills explained that the new music was helping the church expand its reach and suggested the possibility of adjusting the tee time to 12:15 p.m. The man's response was a succinct, "Hell, no."[4] We humans are really good at making things about us, even the worship of Almighty God.

- Danish theologian Søren Kierkegaard likened worship to a drama. It's not (as many assume) that God is the prompter, the pastor and music leaders are the actors, and the congregation is the audience. Rather, the pastor and worship leaders are the prompters, congregants are the actors, and God is the audience.[5] We perform for an audience of One.

Ideas for Preaching on John 20:19-31

When I was sixteen years old and a rising junior, I had pulled back from church (much to the disappointment of my mother). But then, out of sheer spiritual curiosity, I decided to attend a youth retreat. The first night of the retreat, the speaker invited us to write down the thing that was preventing us from committing to Jesus. Without even thinking, I jotted down the word *doubt*. At the time, I believed I was the only person who wrestled with doubt. I later realized I was in good company.

Our text from John is familiar. Thomas is commonly known as "Doubting Thomas," but as John reminds us, his nickname was actually "the twin" (v. 24). John writes more like a poet, so while it is possible that Thomas had a literal twin, the more likely reality is that John is describing Thomas's personality. Simply put, Thomas is a person of two minds. He's like the double-minded person whom James describes (James 1:6-8). There is a part of Thomas that wants to believe, but there is also another part that does not want to risk trusting. The latter part is the part that gives the ultimatum: "Unless I see the nail marks in his hands, put my finger in the wounds left by the nails, and put my hand into his side, I won't believe" (v. 25).

We don't know where Thomas was when the other ten disciples initially encountered the resurrected Christ (vv. 19-23). Still, it's clear that Thomas demands more "proof" than what they experienced. The other ten disciples saw Jesus's wounds (v. 20). However, Thomas wants to physically touch those wounds or will not believe (v. 25).

To be sure, it is not that doubt is bad. For example, in the Gospel of Luke, Simon Peter expresses doubt when Jesus invites him to drop down his nets in deeper water: "Simon replied, 'Master, we've worked hard all night and caught nothing. But because you say so, I'll drop the nets'" (Luke 5:5). The difference between Peter and Thomas are the words, "But because you say so." In other words, Peter still casts down the nets. Thomas, however, by his own admission, will not believe unless he gets the evidence he desires.

Of course, the wonderful thing about all this is that Jesus meets Thomas in his doubt (John 20:27). So too Jesus meets us in our doubt (just like he met me when I was sixteen). We may not receive the same evidence that Thomas did, but we can still join the disciple in conferring to Jesus the divine title, "My Lord and my God" (20:28).

Bringing the Text to Life

- When I think of how Thomas was known as "the twin," I am reminded of the 1988 movie *Twins* starring Arnold Schwarzenegger and Danny DeVito. Just like Schwarzenegger and DeVito could not be more different, Thomas's two minds could not be more different. Consider showing a poster of the film or a side-by-side comparison of the two actors.

- Not all doubt is bad. Have some fun illustrating examples of good doubt. For instance, if somebody randomly emails about a large sum of money they want to deposit in your account, it is good to be doubtful! In my local church, staff and congregants will tell me about emails they receive from individuals posing as me and asking for gift cards. I remind them, when they receive such a message, to doubt that it came from me.

Notes

May 4, 2025–Third Sunday of Easter

Acts 9:1-6, (7-20); *Psalm 30; Revelation 5:11-14;* **John 21:1-19**

Chris Jones

Preacher to Preacher Prayer

Lord God, your love is amazing. You alter our lives and change us, and you gift us with grace that covers and redeems even our worst failures. Thank you for your commitment to us. Help us to faithfully follow where you lead. In the name of Jesus, we pray. Amen.

Ideas for Preaching on Acts 9:1-6, (7-20)

Can people change? Some would say no. Some would say that while we can break certain bad habits and alter small pieces of our personality, radical change is difficult, if not impossible. But the wonderful truth of Easter is that God can change any human life. Nobody in the Bible demonstrates this truth better than Saul.

Formerly the church's worst enemy whose presence must have struck fear and dread in the heart of every Christ-follower, Saul becomes the church's leading apostle. What changed? Simply put, Saul's encounter with the resurrected Jesus.

Saul's transformation was unlikely. It was so unlikely that even Ananias couldn't help but express skepticism: "Lord, I have heard many reports about this man. People say he has done horrible things to your holy people in Jerusalem. He's here with authority from the chief priests to arrest everyone who calls on your name" (vv. 13-14). God doesn't deny the truthfulness of these reports (Saul did do horrible things), but he also reminds Ananias that Saul's story isn't over. Instead, the former persecutor is about to do things that he never imagined (v. 15). In revealing these plans, God announces that Saul isn't just different but radically different, a reality that God himself has authored.

It's remarkable how much God initiates in this story. He initiates the blinding light from heaven and the encounter with Jesus. He initiates Ananias's meeting with Saul. He initiates Saul's future of taking the gospel to Gentiles, kings, and the people of Israel. But above all, he initiates Saul's transformation. Saul didn't change himself. God changed him.

It's hard for people to change, but the God of Easter, who brought forth Jesus from the dead, can change anyone. No one, not even one hellbent on terrorizing Christians, is beyond the grace and power of God.

Bringing the Text to Life

Consider using an example of an unlikely person becoming a Christian. For instance, John Newton was involved in the transatlantic slave trade but, following his conversion to Christianity, felt deep remorse over these actions. Newton became a Church of England clergyman and fierce abolitionist. His hymn "Amazing Grace" highlights the transformation he experienced.

Ideas for Preaching on John 21:1-19

I remember as a college student receiving a phone call that I had been anticipating for weeks. The call was about an opportunity connected to my prospective seminary. I quickly answered the phone and tried to remain calm. "I am sorry to let you know," the caller began, "that you weren't selected." I thanked the person on the other end for letting me know while also trying to hide my disappointment. I felt like a failure.

There are few worse feelings than the feeling that one has failed. However, our passage from John reminds us of the wonderful truth that God is in the business of redeeming failure.

Following the miraculous catch of fish and breakfast on the beach (vv. 1-14), Jesus and Peter share an intimate conversation. Certainly, the experience of having denied Jesus three times must have been weighing on the disciple, but as this scene demonstrates, Jesus's interest is not to condemn, but rather to reinstate. Indeed, this whole scene is set up for Peter's reinstatement. First, Jesus and Peter are sitting by a charcoal fire (v. 8). John reminds us that Peter was by a charcoal fire when he denied Jesus (18:18). Second (and more obvious), the threefold question about love is meant to mirror the threefold denial. Third, Peter had promised to follow Jesus to death (13:37-38), and while he failed to live up to that promise when Jesus was arrested, he would again have that opportunity in the future (18:18-19). In a word, Jesus redeems Peter's failure, transforming it into an opportunity for discipleship.

While some like to make much of the different Greek words for love that show up here (*phileo* versus *agape*), it's important to remember that Jesus and Peter likely shared this conversation in Aramaic. Therefore, instead of focusing on this point, emphasize all the ways this text highlights Jesus's redemptive agenda. We worship a God who refuses to give up on us, who offers grace that covers and redeems even our worse failures.

Bringing the Text to Life

- We usually don't like to advertise our failures, but that is exactly what one man did. Johannes Haushofer, who teaches at Princeton, shocked the social media world in 2016 when he posted a resume of failures. The resume included sections titled "Degree programs I did not get into," "Research funding I did not get," and "Paper rejections from academic journals."[1] Haushofer posted the resume to normalize failure, which everyone, including Peter, Has experienced. However, because of God's grace, our failures don't have the final word.

• The grace Jesus shows Peter reminds me of a story about a promising junior executive at IBM. The young man was involved in a risky venture and ended up losing $10 million of IBM's money in the gamble. He was summoned to the office of Thomas Watson, Sr., who led. "I guess you're calling for my resignation," the man blurted out. "Here it is. I resign effective immediately." Watson laughed. "Resignation? I just spent $10 million dollars training you."[2]

Notes

May 11, 2025–Fourth Sunday of Easter

Acts 9:36-43; Psalm 23; *Revelation 7:9-17; John 10:22-30*

Chris Jones

Preacher to Preacher Prayer

Lord God, thank you for the power of prayer and for using our prayers to enact change. Remind us that you are our Shepherd who loves and cares for us and that you sustain us through hard seasons. We love and praise you. In the name of Jesus, we pray. Amen.

Ideas for Preaching on Acts 9:36-43

Before returning to the Father, Jesus promised the disciples they would do the same, and even greater works than him (John 14:12). In alignment with this commitment, we come to the story of Tabitha's healing.

While Tabitha isn't the first person in Acts to experience miraculous healing, her story certainly stands out. Tabitha was a disciple who had devoted much of her life to helping those in need. But now she stood in need herself, having fallen ill and then dying. That Peter was encouraged to come so quickly signals the belief many had in God's miraculous power: the God who healed people through Jesus could also heal them through the prayers of the apostles. As Peter knelt to pray, it's possible that his mind went back to the scene in Capernaum, where Jesus healed his mother-in-law (Luke 4:38-39). Certainly, the parallel between these stories is worth noting. Both stories are recorded by Luke, and both involve the healing of somebody with a servant's heart (Peter's mother-in-law attended to those in the home as soon as she was healed). Perhaps Peter smiled as he recognized the familiar scene; only this time God's healing power was being carried out through him.

To be sure, such miraculous stories challenge our modern sensibilities— *"People aren't just raised from the dead!"*—so we're tempted to explain them away. Avoid this temptation. Maybe the reason stories like this unsettle us is we've been conditioned to accept decay, disease, and death as the norm rather than putting our faith in the One who, in Jesus and by the power of the Spirit, is sovereign over all these things and, yes, can even overturn them. As Philip Yancey (referencing Jürgen Moltmann) notes, such overturning isn't a suspension of natural laws, but rather a sign of the world as it should be and one day will be when Christ brings all things under his authority.[3]

Bringing the Text to Life

God could have healed Tabitha apart from Peter, but God chose to heal Tabitha through the apostle's prayers. This is a wonderful reminder of God's commitment to using us. However, it is also a reminder of the power of prayer. Karl Barth reportedly said, "*To clasp the hands in prayer* is the beginning of an uprising against the disorder of the world."[4] Tabitha's illness and death were signs of the world's disorder. However, God used Peter's bold prayers to confront this disorder. So too God uses our prayers to confront the disorder of the world.

Ideas for Preaching on Psalm 23

There are few biblical texts as familiar to us as Psalm 23. Many of us memorized this psalm as children. As pastors, we read it aloud in hospital rooms and proclaim its message at funeral services. We find comfort in the psalm's familiarity and the portrait of God it paints.

David likens God to a shepherd, a popular scriptural motif (one that Jesus later uses). In describing God this way, David attributes a number of profound actions to God. What all these actions share—that you will want to emphasize—is they're God-initiated. God lets us rest in grassy meadows, leads us to restful waters, and keeps us alive (v. 2). God guides us in proper paths (v. 3). God protects with his rod and staff (v. 4). God sets a table before us in the presence of our enemies and bathes our head in oil (v. 5). Finally, God pursues us with his goodness and unfailing love (v. 6). We don't perform these actions; rather, they're all initiated by the One whose divine love exceeds understanding.

It's worth noting that David begins the psalm by talking about God (vv. 1-3) but then in verses 4-5 transitions to talking to God directly. Perhaps the reason for the shift is as David describes the most difficult seasons of life (the darkest valley and being in front of one's enemies, seasons with which he was all too familiar), he realizes that theologizing about God won't suffice. Rather, it would be better to speak directly to the One who alone provides protection and blessing that sustains us through such seasons. That's the beauty of Psalm 23; it prompts profound reflection on God and highlights the importance of cultivating a personal relationship with our Shepherd.

Bringing the Text to Life

- The initiative action of God in Psalm 23 illustrates why we baptize babies. Some churches don't baptize babies. However, United Methodists and other churches do partly because we recognize that when we baptize a baby, we catch a glimpse of how all of us are when it comes to God: we are weak, helpless, and in constant need of God's initial (prevenient) grace.

- I love theology. I love reading theological texts and engaging in robust discussions. Thus, I can appreciate the first three verses of Psalm 23, which invite us to think deeply about God. However, my personal relationship with God (cultivated by prayer) has sustained me through difficult life seasons, so I understand why David addresses God in the intimate way that he does in verses 4-5. Consider offering a personal example of how your relationship with the Shepherd has led you through a hard season.

Notes

May 18, 2025–Fifth Sunday of Easter

Acts 11:1-8; Psalm 148; **Revelation 21:1-6; John 13:31-35**

Hugh Hendrickson

Preacher to Preacher Prayer

Almighty God, thank you for your holy scripture and good news of your great love. Help me as I prepare to preach with clarity and conviction about the promises of the new heaven and new earth. I want to experience your holy and endless love this day. Amen.

Ideas for Preaching on Revelation 21:1-6

"Then I saw . . ." As we approach this text, it is crucial to consider the spiritual events John has previously seen in his heavenly vision. Today's lection follows the Final Judgment at the end of the age. John has just seen visions of death and dying. John has seen countless souls cast into a fiery lake where they will experience a second and never-ending death (Revelation 20:11-15).

How quickly the scene changes. Images of death and destruction are now replaced with visions of new things, new spiritual realities. The previous spiritual vision in Revelation 20 focused on the final ending of evil, injustice, and sin. Revelation 21 is about new beginnings. The funeral for the former things concludes, and now we witness a wedding and the loving union of a new heaven and new earth.

Today's text continues into next week. It might be helpful to plan a two-part sermon to unpack all the good news and wonderful promises we find in this passage. A few years ago, I taught, or more accurately tried to teach, a class on Revelation. We used Robert Mulholland's *Journey through the Bible* as our guide and study book. In his commentary on this passage, Mulholland remarked that removing the sea was good news for the Apostle John. John is on Patmos's rocky, isolated island when he experiences his spiritual vision and writes Revelation. The sea might be beautiful, but sadly, the vast sea separated John from his family, friends, and his beloved church family.[5]

The sea is no more. There is no longer a barrier keeping us separated from our holy God. Everything that keeps us from being at home with God is no more. All things are made new. What are the former things or first things that you want to see removed? What barrier from experiencing the fullness of God's love do you long to see removed? Perhaps this is an opportunity to help your hearers consider that heaven isn't just a place we are yearning for. Still, it is also a state of being, a relationship we can obtain through grace and through faith in God.

Bringing the Text to Life

- Display images of sickness, death, disease, doctors, hospitals, and pharmacies and other things that will not be in the new heaven and earth.

- Show some vintage clips of the world of tomorrow. Consider a funny clip of the technology from *The Jetsons.*

- Share promises and predictions of the future. For example: in the 1960s, computers and other office technologies predicted a future office that would be paperless.

Ideas for Preaching on John 13:31-35

"Glory!" Repeated words in the Bible are often important words. In these five verses, variations of the word *glory* appear five times in past and future tense. Glory is translated from the Greek word *doxa.* Glory addresses the character of an object or person. Glory is one of those things that you know when you see it.

In this passage, Jesus is telling us that we will see the glory of God in his passion, suffering, and death. The cruelty and horror of Jesus's death do not necessarily evoke thoughts and images of glory. We tend to think of beautiful, powerful, shiny, and happy things as showing glory. Yet the suffering and death of Jesus genuinely reveal God's beautiful and powerful love in its full glory.

Loving others as Jesus loved us is a glorious thing. Loving with an agape heart is beautiful. Loving like Jesus will mean that the fallen and hurting world can see the glory of God's love in us as faithful disciples. At times, this glory will appear to be cruel and suffering, but if we look closely, we will see the power of God's love in its true beauty. When we love, we glorify God, and God is glorified in us.

For several years, our annual conference was led by a bishop who loved to shout, "Glory, hallelujah!" Bishop Michael B. Watson shouted, "Glory hallelujah!" to identify and acknowledge God's love in action through the ministries of local churches, districts, the annual conference, and the denomination. Where do you see God's love glorified in your life, church, and community? What stirs you to sing the Doxology?

Bringing the Text to Life

- Show photos that capture the glory of nature.

- Ask the congregation to share "glory" sightings. Where have they seen God's glory in their lives?

- Display artwork that shows the passion, suffering, and crucifixion of Jesus.

Notes

May 25, 2025–Sixth Sunday of Easter

Acts 16:9-15; Psalm 67; **Revelation 21:10, 22-22:5; John 14:23-29**

Hugh Hendrickson

Preacher to Preacher Prayer

Gracious God, thank you for the rich heritage of our Wesleyan-Methodist tradition. Bless the preparation and proclamation of your word so the hearers will continue to respond to the good news of your saving grace and love. Amen.

Ideas for Preaching on Revelation 21:10, 22-22:5

In The United Methodist Church, today is Heritage Sunday. Heritage Sunday calls us to remember John Wesley's Aldersgate experience and the rich legacy of our faith tradition. When the first Methodists joined the revival movement that John Wesley led, the only requirement for participation in the worship services and meetings was to express "a desire to flee the wrath to come." This passage does not describe the wrath of God's judgment but rather the blessing for those who have placed their faith in Jesus Christ as Savior and Lord. In today's Gospel reading, John shares a glimpse of the promise Jesus gave his disciples.

John uses rich imagery but fails to fully capture the beauty and wonder that is yet to be. We can only imagine. If only John had a Polaroid camera or Kodachrome film to capture a photo of his spiritual vision. No sermon would be necessary today if we had been blessed with such a photo. We could just stare at the wonderful image and let it speak to us.

But preachers are called to use words to cast a vision and paint a picture of what will be. As I read this lection, I envision a heaven where the place of worship, the temple, is replaced by a person we will worship. Perhaps this reminds us that worship isn't about a place or a building but about people and whom we worship. This new heaven will have no shadows, shade, or darkness. It will also be pure and clean, for there will be no trash or litter. On the surface, this new heaven might seem like a magical kingdom, a destination for vacation and fun, but there is no magic here—only grace and glory!

Bringing the Text to Life

- Show famous pieces of art that depict heaven.

- Show pictures of beautiful landscapes that were ruined by litter.

Ideas for Preaching on John 14:23-29

Today's lesson comes from Jesus's Farwell Discourse. He knows the end is near. Jesus does not have much more time to be with his beloved disciples. Every moment matters.

The Gospel of John begins with a beautiful description of the miracle of Jesus's incarnation. As Jesus prepares to die, to leave, the promise of incarnation not only remains but also becomes a better promise. Jesus leaves them, enabling his heavenly Father to send the Holy Spirit to dwell in us.

For our hearts to be worthy of a home for the Holy Spirit, they must be filled with love for God and God's son. This love is not just a feeling or emotion but an action. The love Jesus speaks of is a verb; it is an action. Love of God is seen through our faithful obedience to Jesus's teaching. When God makes our hearts God's home, we are filled with God's love and perfect peace.

The world we live in continues to need God's love and peace. How can we become a source of God's love and peace where we live? Where is there discord or a lack of peace in your church and community?

Bringing the Text to Life

- Show photos of staged homes for sale and homes that are lived in. Which house is filled with love?

- Show a photo of John Wesley's childhood home in Epworth. Share stories from John and Charles's childhood.

Notes

June 1, 2025–Ascension of the Lord

Acts 1:1-11; *Psalm 47 or Psalm 93;* **Ephesians 1:15-23;** *Luke 24:44-53*

Hugh Hendrickson

Preacher to Preacher Prayer

You alone are the Lord, the Most High. You are awesome and the great king over all the earth. As I prepare to preach this week, help me to stand in awe of your grace and love. Fill my heart with joy so I can truly bring the good news to your people. Amen.

Ideas for Preaching on Acts 1:1-11

Forty days after Easter, the church celebrates the Ascension of the Lord. Forty days after Easter falls on a Thursday, so it is customary for congregations to celebrate the Ascension of the Lord on the following Sunday. It might be worth noting that Jesus returned to the glory of heaven on a Thursday so we could experience the grace of heaven on Sunday. Suppose your congregation does not observe this holy day. In that case, I highly encourage you to do so, for the Ascension of the Lord fulfills many of Jesus's wonderful promises made to his disciples and the church.

Acts is a continuation of the Gospel of Luke. This text closely parallels today's Gospel lection from Luke 24:44-53. It could be helpful to compare and contrast Acts 1:1-11 with Luke 24:44-53. Jesus's ministry has not changed. Even after his resurrection, Jesus still teaches about the kingdom of God.

Did you notice that even after the resurrection of Jesus and spending forty days with the risen Christ, the disciples still fail to comprehend his teaching about the coming kingdom of God? Sadly, they still seem to think that Jesus will restore Israel to its former glory. Their minds are still fixed on the past when God is moving forward in fulfilling the baptism and outpouring of the Holy Spirit. How often do we want God to restore the past and its remembered glory? What would it mean for us to trust the Holy Spirit to lead us to the promise of something new? Are we willing to wait until we receive the promise before we head out on mission and ministry to the ends of the earth?

When I was in seminary, my friends would discuss various topics around the lunch table in the cafeteria. One day, I tried to stir conversation by asking my friends, "What do you think was the best thing Jesus ever said?" Someone quoted John 3:16;

another said, "Love one another." Another friend debated if it was even possible to rank Jesus's words. Then my Bulgarian friend, Miroslav, chimed in, "I do not know what the best thing Jesus said was, but I do know what was the last thing Jesus said, 'You will receive power when the Holy Spirit comes upon you; and you will be my witnesses in Jerusalem, in all Judea and Samaria, and to the ends of the earth.'" We don't know the best thing Jesus said, but yes, we know the last thing he said.

Bringing the Text to Life

*   Show clips of people having a hard time waiting.

*   I know this is ridiculous, but I always thought it would be cool to have a hot air balloon offer free rides for the church and community to celebrate the Ascension.

*   Show a video of the spread of the church from Jerusalem across the world to today.

Ideas for Preaching on Ephesians 1:15-23

This passage of scripture comes at the end of Paul's lengthy and complex sentence that followed his words of greeting to the Ephesians. Paul is sharing his prayer for the church. When we remember that Paul entered the church's story as Saul, the persecutor of the church, we can see the transforming power of God's grace. Paul prays for the church to experience and grow in what he has experienced, the transforming power of God's holy love and grace.

We tend to think of grace in the sense of the gift of God's love. However, grace is more than God's holy love. Grace is an enabling power. Grace enables us to do what Jesus did, and grace empowers us to do what Jesus has called us to do. For us to be faithful and fruitful disciples and for the church to indeed be the body of Christ, we need God's grace.

Paul explains that we can receive the gift of God's grace because Christ has ascended to his heavenly place at the right hand of God. The Ascension is a fundamental doctrine that affects our daily lives. It is customary for many churches to affirm this spiritual truth when they recite the Apostles' Creed in their worship services, but do we understand the significance of what the ascended Christ is doing at the right hand of God?

Jesus's ministry has not changed, only the location of that ministry. Jesus is still preaching and teaching about the kingdom of God. As our great high priest, Jesus is interceding for his disciples. Jesus is gifting us the benefits of his righteousness so we can be filled with the Holy Spirit and be empowered by God's grace. The ascended Christ is giving us revelation and wisdom. We can know the truth and apply the truth to our lives. The ascended Christ is opening our eyes and helping us to see. We are granted spiritual vision so we can see the work of God's power and God's kingdom growing around us. Christ is working for our benefit in heaven so we can minister for him on earth.

Bringing the Text to Life

- What do people hear about your congregation? What are people saying about your church? If you have social media reviews, it might be appropriate to share them.

- Ask people to share what they are thankful for about your church.

- Set up a prayer board for people to write down prayer requests.

Notes

June 8, 2025–Day of Pentecost

Acts 2:1-21; Psalm 104:24-34, 35b; Romans 8:14-17;
John 14:8-17, (25-27)

Hugh Hendrickson

Preacher to Preacher Prayer

Come, Holy Spirit. Set my heart aflame with the fire of your pure love. Quicken my spirit and help me to proclaim your good news with a Pentecostal boldness like Peter when he preached the first sermon for Christ's church. Amen.

Ideas for Preaching on Acts 2:1-21

Today is Pentecost. Fifty days ago, the church was gathered to celebrate the resurrection of Jesus from the dead on Easter Sunday. Today, we celebrate the outpouring of the Holy Spirit on the disciples and faithful gathered in Jerusalem. Fifty days ago, the disciples hid behind locked doors and windows because they feared that the same religious and political authorities who executed Jesus would soon come to execute them. Ten days ago, the disciples watched Jesus ascend into the heavens and take his place at the right hand of God the Father.

I don't know about you, but there are times when I want the church to change quickly. Any significant change in the church is a miracle of God's grace. Yet in the course of fifty days, the disciples go from hiding in a spirit of fear in the Upper Room to going out from the Upper Room empowered and full of faith to continue Jesus's ministry and transform the world as they seek the kingdom of God. What is the source of this change? The Holy Spirit, the fullness of God living in us through our faith in Jesus Christ. What would happen if we truly opened our hearts to the fullness of God's presence and power through the indwelling of the Holy Spirit? If we opened our lives to the Holy Spirit, what new language of God's goodness, love, and power would we be able to proclaim?

For many years, I wondered why Luke specifically mentioned the people and places present in Jerusalem on the day of Pentecost. One day, I decided to look up the regions listed in Acts 2 on the maps in the back of my Bible. It just happened that the map I was using had the missionary journeys of Paul and the early church charted on it. It looked like God was playing connect the dots. In the Wesleyan/Methodist tradition, we might consider this an example of prevenient grace. God had people in Jerusalem present for Pentecost. They went home with a firsthand account of what transpired. In a few years, when Paul and the early church missionaries showed up with the good news of the gospel, there were people in the community who could bear witness and affirm their testimony about Pentecost. How might God connect the dots for your church to do great things for the kingdom?

Bringing the Text to Life

- Have people read the scripture in their native tongue. If possible, include American Sign Language.

- Display a map that helps hearers locate the regions listed in Acts 2. You could also show the overlay of the growth of the early church.

- Show artistic depictions of Pentecost.

Ideas for Preaching on John 14:8-17, (25-27)

The conversation in our passage likely occurred in the Upper Room fifty-one days before Pentecost. It is Maundy Thursday. Jesus will soon die on the cross on Good Friday. I wonder if the house owner who let Jesus and his disciples use the Upper Room had a clue that this space would be the location of such significant, world-changing spiritual events. Have you ever considered the life-changing and perhaps world-changing spiritual events in your sanctuary?

The conversation in our passage is part of Jesus's farewell discourse. This is Jesus's last lecture to his disciples before he is crucified. I wonder if Philip's question disappointed Jesus. Philip enters the story of Jesus's ministry in John 1:43. Jesus finds him and invites Philip to follow him. Philip invites Nathaniel to "come and see." The last time Philip speaks in John, he asks Jesus to show them the Father. For Philip, seeing is believing. Jesus seems to be worried about Philip's vision and his attention. "Philip, what have you been doing these last three years? Have you been asleep? Have you even been paying attention?"

Now, it is time for the disciples to put their faith into action truly. They need to remember what they have seen Jesus do and trust in Jesus to help them do even greater things. These greater things will be possible because of the atoning work of Jesus's death and resurrection. Jesus's agape love for the world will become the means by which we will be empowered by agape love to do great things for God's glory and God's kingdom. Hold on, church, "you ain't seen nothing yet!"

Jesus offers us endless possibilities of power through faithful love. Such promises of greater things might scare us, but Jesus says there is nothing to worry about because he will be with us, and his presence will bring us true peace. Jesus has come to the world and given the God of love a face. Pentecost empowers us to go into the world, demonstrating God's love. Perhaps it would be a breath of fresh air to encourage your hearers to think about the endless possibilities of God's love at work in and through us.

Bringing the Text to Life

- If people look at your life, what image of God would they see? What understanding of God's love would they have from your witness?

- Ask the congregation to share God-sized dreams of greater things that the church can do through the work of the Holy Spirit.

- Share pictures of places where several historic events have occurred: the National Mall in Washington D.C., famous sports arenas, or local landmarks.

Notes

June 15, 2025–Trinity Sunday

Proverbs 8:1-4, 22-31; Psalm 8; **Romans 5:1-5; John 16:12-15**

Hugh Hendrickson

Preacher to Preacher Prayer

Almighty and everlasting God, grant me the grace to proclaim, better understand, and experience the beautiful mystery of the Holy Trinity. Empower me through the Holy Spirit to help people experience the glory and love of the Father through the good news of Jesus Christ. Amen.

Ideas for Preaching on Romans 5:1-5

On the liturgical calendar, today is Trinity Sunday. Last week, the church celebrated its birth and the outpouring of the Holy Spirit on Pentecost. Today, we are invited to celebrate the mysterious, beautiful, and holy union of God's loving fullness as Father, Son, and Holy Spirit. To be honest, most people in the pew won't know it is Trinity Sunday. In further honesty, most laity and clergy have difficulty explaining the Holy Trinity without straying into some trinitarian heresy.

In today's lection from Romans 5, Paul continues his explanation of God's plan of redemption through the Old Testament into the present age of the church. Paul explains God's plan of salvation from the days of Abraham to Jesus. God's work of redemption is all of God's doing. There is nothing we can do to earn this gift of forgiving grace other than placing our trust in God's saving work through faith in his son, Jesus. The Holy Spirit enables us to know and experience the gift of God's love.

Perhaps the most helpful way to craft a sermon on this passage would be to use it as an invitation to simply remember and marvel at the wondrous ways God has extended grace upon grace to us through God's holy love. It is hard to truly fathom what God has done for us since the garden of Eden, the days of Abraham, and the ministry of Jesus. Faith in Jesus brings us into the glorious and beautiful mystery of the Trinity. We can experience God's holy love here and now amid the suffering and pain of our fallen world. We are also encouraged to focus on the future promise of fully being incorporated into the holy union of the Trinity in the new heaven and earth at the age of the age.

The God who made us, the God we rebelled against, is the God who has come to us, the God who died for us, the God who lives for us, the God who is now with us, and the God who will bring us to our eternal home. This is the glorious, good news of God's grace. This promise will help us become the people of grace that God desires us to be.

Bringing the Text to Life

- This passage speaks of endurance-producing character. If you have someone in your congregation or community who has endured difficulty, their testimony could help bring the promise of hope to life.

- Be careful using illustrations like ice, water, steam, or an egg to explain the Trinity. Reciting the Nicene Creed to better understand the Trinity might be more helpful.

Ideas for Preaching on John 16:12-15

The Trinity has been a challenge for many Christians to understand. The triune essence of God as Father, Son, and Holy Spirit is simple but quite complex. Attempts to explain the Trinity with symbols and analogies can easily drift into trinitarian heresies such as Modalism and Tritheism. Passages like this reading from John 16 aren't necessarily helpful.

Today's scripture is from Jesus's Farewell Discourse. Jesus is sharing from his heart to the hearts of his disciples as they are in the Upper Room. Jesus has washed their feet and served them Holy Communion. He has told them he is about to leave them. Jesus knows his death is imminent.

The disciples have already shown Jesus that they do not understand what being the Messiah requires of him. They are not expecting that he will die. It seems that they believed Jesus was going to leave on a trip or another mission. Jesus is heading to the cross and the pits of hell. This is a journey the disciples are unable to make. But Jesus's passion and death are central to God's glorious plan of redemption.

God the Father, God the Son, and God the Spirit all work together to redeem us. This is the beauty of the Trinity. This is a movement of grace, mercy, and love. Some theologians have called this a divine dance. I am not a dancer, but I've been to many dances. Last year, my niece got married. I watched her dance with her father, and I watched her dance with her husband. They whispered as they moved along the dance floor, close to each other in a loving embrace. I couldn't hear what was said, but I knew a message of love was shared between the two.

The Holy Spirit is bringing us into the sacred and holy dance of the Trinity. The Holy Spirit, as the spirit of truth, will connect our hearts with the heart of God. In that loving conversation, we will experience God's union of holiness, and the mystery of God's glory will begin to make sense to us.

What would it look like for your church to enter a dance with God? What truth is God trying to speak to you and your church? How does this truth help you understand God's glorious plan of redemption? How does this truth stand up in a world of spiritual misinformation?

Bringing the Text to Life

- Consider showing a video clip of a father and daughter dance or a husband and wife dance at a wedding.

- Find images of trinitarian icons and use them to prompt discussion. Ask people what they see. What do they think the pictures symbolize?

- Play video clips of people speaking without sound and see if people know what is being said. This draws upon the idea that the Spirit will help us understand what God and Jesus have discussed in heaven.

Notes

June 22, 2025–Second Sunday after Pentecost

1 Kings 19:1-4, (5-7), 8-15a; Psalm 42 and 43; Isaiah 65:1-9; Psalm 22:19-28; Galatians 3:23-29; Luke 8:26-39

Pam McCurdy

Preacher to Preacher Prayer

Dear God, thank you for these scriptures and the opportunity to sit with them awhile. Guide us in the process of pondering, planning, and preaching. Amen.

Ideas for Preaching on 1 Kings 19:1-4, (5-7), 8-15a

After reading the featured scripture, it is clear that Elijah is having a bad day. Elijah has zealously called out King Ahab and the nation of Israel for turning from a covenant relationship with God to the worship of Baal. Today's scripture makes it plain that Elijah's zeal might result in his death, but that God has the prophet's back.

Angered by Israel's apostasy, God has Elijah tell Ahab that a drought will hit the land. For three years not one drop of rain or dew falls on the land of Israel. Next, Elijah challenges the Priest of Baal to a showdown. The god who shows up and shows out by consuming a sacrifice with fire is indeed God. Baal is a no-show, but God does not fail to answer Elijah's prayer. When Elijah kills all the prophets of Baal and word gets back to Jezebel, she is more than angry. She is set on revenge and Elijah is the target.

Out of fear, Elijah flees for his life. Now, we might be prone to judge Elijah for his lack of trust in God. After all, God has sustained Elijah's life by providing food, water, and shelter in amazing ways. God has made God's presence and power known.

Fear has a way of stalling our ability to think rationally and memory fails us. Survival mode kicks in and we do what we think is necessary in the moment. This is not necessarily a bad thing. Can we really blame Elijah for putting some distance between himself and Jezebel? There are occasions when we must retreat to safety. We all face events that elicit reactions of fear. Sometimes, we need a safe space to acknowledge our confusion, frustration, and fear. We need time for physical, mental, emotional, and spiritual rest.

God does not berate Elijah for giving up. God takes care of Elijah's physical needs. God asks Elijah this question, "What are you doing here?" and gives an opportunity for Elijah to tell his story and name his fear. God brings comfort to Elijah with a face-to-face meeting. It is unexpectantly silent but powerful. God continues to show up for Elijah. God will show up for us.

Bringing the Text to Life

- You cannot gloss over the reality of fear-inducing experiences in life, so acknowledge it.

- Assure your congregation that it is okay to express deep emotions and concerns to God.

- Proclaim that God is faithful and provides what God knows we need when we need it.

- Create an altar scape of various types of bread and containers of water displayed among rocks.

- Ask the choir to sing "God Will Provide" by Mark Patterson as the anthem.

- Show pictures of the Judean wilderness, a broom tree, and Mt. Horeb.

- As you read the scripture, take an intended pause for silence between verses twelve and thirteen.

- Share stories of God comforting someone dealing with fear.

Ideas for Preaching Psalm 42 and 43

The summer heat has been unbearable. It is miserably humid and the air feels so thick that it is hard to breath. I don't recall a summer where I have ever felt so uncomfortable and been so thirsty. My green insulated cup filled with cold water is an everyday accessory because water is the only thing that quenches my physical thirst and brings relief.

The psalmist knows about thirst. It is a soul thirst. So desperate is their need for hope that their soul longs for God's presence and hope. Enemies oppress and adversaries taunt the psalmist with "Where's your God now?" (42:3). The psalmist calls out to God with similar questions, "Why have you forgotten me?" and "Why have you rejected me?" (42:9; 43:2). There is a sense of abandonment in these questions, which is relatable.

Where is God when a terminal diagnosis is given, a loved one dies, or a relationship ends? Where is God when we work so hard but the money does not stretch? Where is God when "isms" and "phobias" result in growing hate and violence in our country and throughout the world? Where is God when we, like the psalmist, thirst for hope?

Something within the psalmist takes them back to the God they know and have experienced. They have memories of what it is to put hope in God. They have experiences of God's presence and steadfast love. They have known God as their rock and place of refuge. It is these memories of hope fulfilled by God that allows the psalmist to hold on to hope in the present. God has been and will be their help. Remembrance leads to renewed hope. Renewed hope will lead to praise.

Bringing the Text to Life

- How does the experience of the psalmist relate to the distress or trouble your congregation or community is experiencing?

- Consider what folks are thirsting for in life.

- What is hope? What is hope in God?

- Consider the use of memory in the scripture and how God's people are called to remember God's activity. What role does memory play in producing hope? Renewing hope?

- Cover the altar in flowing fabrics in different shades of blue to represent a flowing stream.

- Play the sound of flowing water before the scripture is read.

- Share memories of how God renewed your hope or someone else's.

- Pass out refillable water bottles at the end of the service as a reminder that God can quench our thirsty souls.

Notes

June 29, 2025–Third Sunday after Pentecost

2 Kings 2:1-2, 6-14; *Psalm 77:1-2, 11-20; 1 Kings 19:15-16, 19-21;
Psalm 16;* **Galatians 5:1, 13-25**; *Luke 9:51-62*

Pam McCurdy

Preacher to Preacher Prayer

*Dear God, thank you for these scriptures and the opportunity to sit with them awhile.
Guide us in the process of pondering, planning, and preaching. Amen.*

Ideas for Preaching on 2 Kings 2:1-2, 6-14

The prophet Elijah and his disciple, Elisha, have journeyed together. Elisha has witnessed Elijah speak God's words to the kings of Israel. In today's text, Elisha will witness the departure of his master and mentor, Elijah. However, the incredible departure of Elijah does not happen until the prophet passes his mantle on to Elisha.

Elijah has nurtured and taught Elisha and it is time for his student to carry on the work. It is time to pass on the mantle, which is more than a garment for warmth. It is a visible sign of authority. Elijah knows the rewards and the risks of being a prophet, so before passing his mantle, he asks Elisha what he can do for him.

What an incredibly significant and wise request Elisha makes in asking for a double share of Elijah's spirit. The student knows from observation that the work of being a prophet for God is not easy and that one needs to be equipped for it. Elijah has set the standard and Elisha wants to meet it. Elisha's request is granted as the spirit of Elijah rests on him. Prophetic work, on behalf of God, will continue through Elisha.

One of the essential tasks of being clergy is to encourage disciples of Jesus Christ to grow in and live out their faith. One of the most beautiful experiences is to witness this growth. Directed by the Holy Spirit, we guide disciples through our ministry. Along with the laity, we nurture them, pray for them, and challenge them. Hopefully, we set an example for them. Yes, we want these disciples to experience the joy of knowing Jesus, but for the growth of God's kingdom, we urge and help equip them to carry out their ministry tasks. Proclaiming the good news of Jesus Christ must continue.

One of the greatest privileges I have is to journey with and mentor individuals exploring a call to ministry in The United Methodist Church. For me this task is a way of thanking those who nurtured me in the faith and those who passed the mantle of ministry on to me.

Bringing the Text to Life

- To give some background, consider briefly sharing how Elisha became a disciple of Elijah from 1 Kings 19:19-21.

- What does "passing the mantle" mean in your congregation? How is this accomplished? How does it support your church's ongoing ministry of proclaiming the gospel inside and outside the church?

- In your context, how does this scripture highlight and encourage ministry with children and youth within the church and in the surrounding community?

- Share stories of being mentored or of mentoring. This can be your own story or that of someone else.

- Share your story of being called, commissioned, or ordained to ministry.

- If your UMC Conference has a Passing of Mantle Service, share the details and how this event relates to your own ministry journey.

- If you wear a stole, explain its significance. Use your stole or stoles as a prop.

- Is there an item that has been passed down to you that is special to you? If so, use it as a prop. Why were you the recipient? Do you have plans to pass it on?

Ideas for Preaching on Galatians 5:1, 13-25

In his letter to the Galatians, Paul argues against false teaching that requires Christians of Galatia to be circumcised and to the follow the law. Paul reminds the Galatians that their righteousness is not secured by strict adherence of the law. In Christ, the Galatians are free. Paul assures them that all Christians—whether they are Gentiles or Jews—are seen as righteous before God through their acceptance of and faith in the person and work of Jesus Christ. This is the gospel Paul proclaimed to the Galatians from the beginning, and it still holds true. The Galatians must not follow other gospels being taught.

What does it look for the Galatian Christian to live into this freedom given to them by Christ? Paul shares with them that by seeking and following the guidance of the Holy Spirit, they will use this freedom to live a life marked by loving their neighbor as they love themselves. However, he also warns the Galatians that this freedom is not an invitation to wreak havoc and harm on oneself or their neighbor.

Paul provides them with a list, in case they need clarification, on behaviors to avoid and behaviors to practice.

The Christians of Galatia are to be known by love, joy, peace, patience, kindness, generosity, faithfulness, gentleness, and self-control. What was true for those early Christians remains true for us, today.

Bringing the Text to Life

* What is it to be seen as righteous or justified before God? How does grace play into it?

* What extra requirements do some Christians place on being a Christian? Why?

* What difference can it make to someone if they know they can come to Christ without "jumping through hoops"?

* What is the difference between the secular meaning of freedom and the freedom that Christ gives?

* How would the world look if your congregation lives out the fruit of the Spirit?

* Create a banner that lists the fruit of the Spirit.

* Create an altar scape with colorful cloth and baskets of fruit.

* Create and show a video of members of the congregation or community sharing the meaning of each fruit of the Spirit.

* Share stories of how the freedom that Christ gives has changed someone's life.

Notes

July 6, 2025–Fourth Sunday after Pentecost

2 Kings 5:1-14; *Psalm 30; Isaiah 66:10-14; Psalm 16;*
Galatians 6:(1-6), 7-16; Luke 10:1-11,16-20

Pam McCurdy

Preacher to Preacher Prayer

Dear God, thank you for these scriptures and the opportunity to sit with them awhile. Guide us in the process of pondering, planning, and preaching. Amen

Ideas for Preaching on 2 Kings 5:1-14

It is surprising that the commander of an army would take the advice of his servant girl, but Naaman does. The king of Israel is surprised by the king of Aram's sending Naaman to Samaria for a cure for leprosy. Naaman is a great man who led Aram's army to victories, so something is suspicious.

Naaman is surprised and angry when Elisha does not personally appear before him but sends a messenger with instructions. There is no Elijah calling on God or waving his hands over Naaman. There is no need for Elisha to be physically present. God is with Naaman and that's all it takes. The prophet's simple instruction to wash seven times in the Jordan River works and Naaman is surprised and pleased. Later in the chapter, Naaman proclaims the God of Israel as the only god.

It is no surprise that the king of Aram would give Naaman permission to go to Israel to find a cure for his leprosy. After all, Naaman has delivered the king many victories. Naaman is highly favored, and the king needs his military skills.

It is no surprise to Elisha that Naaman is cured of his leprosy, because God is in control. Elisha knows about the power of God. The prophet has witnessed God at work.

Our loving God is still at work, so we should not be surprised at God's activity. What often surprises us are the ways in which God works. Unfortunately, we are often surprised, disappointed, and uncomfortable when God works for the good of people we disapprove of or cast off as unworthy.

We would do well to learn a lesson from Elisha. Neither Naaman's nationality nor his prestige mattered to Elisha. Naaman was in need. God could cure disease.

Naaman's experience of God's healing power changed him physically and spiritually. Perhaps our trust in God and our response to people's needs will bring about surprising change.

Bringing the Text to Life

- Where is God at work in your congregation and community?

- Are you surprised by how God is working and with whom God is working? Is the congregation surprised?

- What are the needs of your community? Is your congregation responding to them? If yes, why? If no, why not?

- What lessons can your congregation learn from Elisha's response to Naaman?

- What lessons can your congregation learn from God's response to Naaman?

- Display photos of your community.

- Display photos of your congregation in ministry in the community.

- Share stories of lives that have been changed by God working through the hands and feet of Christians. If there are stories from your context, use those.

- Share stories of how Christians have been changed because of their ministry with others. If there are stories from your context, use those.

- What are the needs of your community? Share this information with your congregation. Share visions of what God can do through your congregation. Dream.

- Address the reason for hesitation to help and share how to filter those reasons through the lens of Christ calling us to love our neighbor as ourselves.

Ideas for Preaching on Galatians 6:(1-6), 7-16

In reading this text the phrase "Mind your own business" comes to mind. Yes, Christians are to hold one another accountable. We pray for one another. We encourage and support one another. We gently offer words of concern and correction. In pointing out the faults of others, how many fingers are pointing back at us? We have to keep our own words and actions in check.

In verse seven, Paul says we reap what we sow. Choices have consequences, so what is the outcome of our words and actions? Are we paying attention to the leading of the Holy Spirit?

Do we keep in mind Paul's encouragement in verse 10, "Let's work for the good of all whenever we have an opportunity and especially for those in the household of faith"?

Paul also reminds us that through a relationship with Jesus Christ, we are new creations. This marks our identity. Our thinking is to reflect it. Our words and actions are to reflect it.

How does what we have sown reflect that we are disciples of Christ? How does what we have sown corporately reflect that we are the body of Christ?

Bringing the Text to Life

- What does it mean to be a "new creation"?

- Why and how do Christians hold one another accountable?

- What instructions does John Wesley give for small groups and accountability?

- How can this accountability be a positive or negative experience?

- How can we be attuned to the leading of the Holy Spirit when it comes to what we "sow" and what we "reap"? Is this a place to mention the fruit of the Spirit?

- What is your congregation sowing and reaping through its words and actions?

- What can your congregation sow and reap? What is the congregation's dream or vision for reaping a harvest for Jesus Christ? How will it transform them and the community?

- Share stories of the positive effects of accountability groups done correctly.

- Address the reasons why we tend to point fingers at other folk, but ignore our own faults.

- Create an altar scape that visualizes planting, growing, and reaping a harvest.

- Briefly share the process of planting, growing, and harvesting.

- If you reference the fruits of the Spirit and have a banner displaying them, use the banner in this service.

- Share stories of how "work for the good of all" makes a difference.

Notes

July 13, 2025–Fifth Sunday after Pentecost

Amos 7:7-17; Psalm 82; **Deuteronomy 30:9-14**; *Psalm 25:1-10;
Colossians 1:1-14;* **Luke 10:25-37**

Lisa Yebuah

Preacher to Preacher Prayer

Gracious God, your love buoys our work and carries our words. Breathe upon the scriptures now and breathe upon our hearts. May our worship-full preparation tether itself to your Word and be near to us, in our mouths, and etched on our hearts.

Ideas for Preaching on Deuteronomy 30:9-14

At first glance, the appointed text starts at an awkward place; however, the underlying message does not feel confusing or disruptive. Verse 9 begins a beautiful declaration of God's goodness and generous blessing in all aspects of human life. God delights in abundance, and because of who God is, there will be tangible markers of God's hand at work in one's family, among their livestock, and reflected in overflowing harvest. Essentially, life will be good! This verse, in particular, provides an opportunity to reframe the words *prosper* and *prosperity*, which can sometimes be used in harmful ways. Prosperity, then, can find itself situated within the framework of God's economy, a way of being that is not thwarted by scarcity but is wed to flourishing.

It behooves the preacher to remind the hearers that God's desire "to make you abundantly prosperous in all your undertakings" is connected to a grander context and narrative portraying the covenant love of God. Covenant underscores the relational dynamic between the divine and humanity. In fact, connecting all five verses within the pericope to this meta-narrative of Deuteronomy is not only a wise move, but it is also a hospitable one, especially when navigating the conditional statement in verse 10. We should always return to this truth: God's fidelity does not waver even when humanity is fickle or faithless.

Keeping the commandments, holding onto God's decrees, and turning wholly to God are crucial to the personal and communal formation of God's people, but these human gestures do not ultimately make or break the Lord's commitment to God's created. Therein is the underlying grace when the commandments feel too difficult or too far off as depicted in the celestial and sea imagery used in verses 11-13. This voice in Deuteronomy invites us to have an imagination for a close-to-us-law, a word so near it makes a home in our hearts. What a gift!

Bringing the Text to Life

It can be challenging to conceptualize a text when it speaks to realities like commandments or the law. However, an open Bible prominently placed at a main entrance could signal… Embodied practices might also work to bring this passage to life. As the scripture is read, consider inviting the congregation to take on one of these postures: holding hands open (v. 9) or placing hands over the heart (v. 14).

Ideas for Preaching on Luke 10:25-37

It will be important to use holy restraint when unearthing this text because the parable of the good Samaritan offers no shortage of possible directions a preacher could take. If you attempt (or feel pressure) to say everything, you might run the risk of becoming reductive in how you describe the various characters within this story, or you might perpetuate caricatures of groups of people, or your language might sound too much like modern-day "us versus them" rhetoric. Our role is to undo unhelpful binaries, not affirm them.

Ironically, naming the pitfalls can be a direction for the sermon. You can name what happens when we overlook the nuance and beautiful complexity of people's identities, social location, and perspectives. You can acknowledge how we miss out on the ever-expansive messages Jesus provides through the use of parables. Jesus leaves room for us to see beyond what we can see in each other. How do we see people injured and harmed by systems? How do we see those who harm and who participate in systems of oppression? How do we see religious institutions and figures? How do we see people whose humanity is not even acknowledged unless first qualified with the word "good"? How do we see ourselves when we can or cannot see our neighbors rightly? Asking these questions speaks to the message underneath this narrative.

If you sense a call to explore the various characters in the text, consider focusing on only one character and then posing a point and counterpoint with your focus. For example, if you were to preach about the wounded person who was left for dead, you could acknowledge how powerful it is for this person to be cared for by another and what a gift that their pain was not dismissed by the Samaritan. Additionally, you could preach about the grand nature of trust displayed when the wounded person allowed themselves to be cared for, especially after a moment of great injury.

Bringing the Text to Life

- Show a slideshow of newspaper headlines describing local heroes as "good Samaritans."
- Display a copy of Paulus Hoffman's "good Samaritan" painting.
- Tell a story when the word *good* was not helpful or was very helpful.

Notes

July 20, 2025–Sixth Sunday after Pentecost

Amos 8:1-12; Psalm 52; **Genesis 18:1-10a**; Psalm 15; Colossians
1:15-28; **Luke 10:38-42**

Lisa Yebuah

Preacher to Preacher Prayer

Lord, we give you thanks for the ways your divine presence shows up in the ordinary. Like Abraham, allow us to see realities beyond the words we see. Illumine the texts and keep us present to what they unearth in us.

Ideas for Preaching on Genesis 18:1-10a

The tension in preaching this portion of Genesis 18 is that we know the end of the story and the impact of Sarah's response (laughing at God), yet this pericope does not actually introduce us to Sarah beyond her role behind the scenes. She is spoken about. She is spoken to. But Sarah is not given voice to speak about herself or to speak to these divine strangers who meet her husband under the oaks at Mamre. However, we have a unique starting place, working our way from the end. Verse 10a gives us this promise: "I will definitely return to you about this time next year. Then your wife Sarah will have a son." We are not yet privy to Sarah's response to this too-good-to-be-true message, but we are given a glimpse into the grace that is felt when a word of promise is shared in the midst of a barren situation. "In due season" is not a suggestion. It is tied to a God who breaks into time.

Additionally, the set-up to the words of promise holds a variety of opportunities and on-ramps for the preacher to take. One might consider how Abraham's posture sitting at the tent entrance presents powerful examples for how the hearers of the Word might position themselves in life. While sitting in the heat of the day, Abraham has an encounter with God. Three men, who are understood to be messengers of God, approach Abraham. Abraham's worshipful response testifies to his keen awareness that these men are more than what the human eyes can see. Abraham's attentiveness is on full display. So, too, can people of faith be invited to practice holy awareness wherein we keep ourselves open to seeing the extraordinary in the ordinary. Similarly, the way Abraham attends to these strangers speaks to how we are called to attend to whatever is before us, trusting that there is something lovely about the people, circumstances, messages, or realities God sends our way. Lastly, Abraham receives the promise without protesting or questioning. It is as though hearing the words is enough for Abraham to trust in the unfolding of a miracle.

So where might we encounter God? Abraham was sitting at the entrance of a tent. Maybe your congregants will find themselves sitting in the car, or at a desk, or on a pew when the Lord appears? Wherever they are, will they be open to seeing the divine and to believing in promises unfolding?

Bringing the Text to Life

- Tell a story about someone who spoke a God-good work over you.

- Invite congregants into a guided meditation while they are sitting in their seats/pews.

- Teach on the examen or some other spiritual practice that sharpens our awareness.

Ideas for Preaching on Luke 10:38-42

It is helpful to resist the temptation of speaking about Mary and Martha within an either/or paradigm. In doing so, we can create a false dichotomy between these two sisters. Something to keep in mind is that, at any point in our lives, we might resemble a Mary-like posture or a Martha-like posture or a bit of both sisters at the same time. The preacher of this text could point to other pairs in scripture that show us the expanse of our humanity and the range of our human responses. For instance, sometimes we are called to let go like Orpah, and sometimes we are called to cling like Ruth. One action is not inherently better than the other, though in context, one character might shed light on some aspect of faithfulness we sense is the highest good to center in our preaching. That is understandable as long as we do not speak about Martha and Mary in hyperbole or with absolutes.

This passage has a progression that can be teased out for congregants. Martha welcomes Jesus into her home while Mary welcomes and is attentive to Jesus's presence. Martha centers her tasks while Jesus invites her to center his presence. What should not be glossed over is the first move of hospitality; it rests with Martha's invitation. She initially makes space for Jesus. How quickly we forget how Martha's gesture of invitation is what draws Jesus into her home! Maybe it would be fair to Martha's character to remind ourselves that she is not the "bad guy." Hard stop. She is human. Hard stop. This is a beautiful point to uplift, because Martha's latter distracted state should not carte blanche discount or discredit her initial faithful attempts.

However, Martha's focus on her home tasks and Mary's presence to Christ's presence reveal how distractions can derail us from being attentive to God at work and how we have the capacity to be present to the divine. Unlike Mary (or Abraham in Genesis 18), Martha cannot see beyond what she can tangibly direct her attention. She misses out on Jesus in her midst, though he is at hand, within arm's reach. If most people are honest, we can confess how we live perpetually distracted lives. The tyranny of busy-ness, our overloaded calendars, our overthinking, and our over-functioning keep us from being present to ourselves, present to others, or present to God. We are human. Hard stop. Thankfully, Jesus does not meet Martha with rebuke, but instead, with an invitation to a better reality, a greater reality, to be attentive to God made flesh in her home.

Bringing the Text to Life

- Invite congregants to write down on notecards things that distract them or take their focus away from Jesus.

- Consider sitting in silence for one minute following the sermon as a means of "practicing the presence."

- Share when you have been like Mary and when you have also been like Martha.

- Invite reflection about shelter-in-place during the pandemic. Ask what distractions did we recognize were real when they were stripped away from us.

Notes

July 27, 2025–Seventh Sunday after Pentecost

*Hosea 1:2-10; Psalm 85; **Genesis 18:20-32**; Psalm 138; Colossians 2:6-15, (16-19); **Luke 11:1-13***

Rachel Cornwell

Preacher to Preacher Prayer

God our Father, our Mother, enlighten and inspire those who preach your Word to offer hope and spiritual sustenance to your church and the world. Amen.

Ideas for Preaching on Genesis 18:20-32

The story of Sodom (and her sister city Gomorrah) from the book of Genesis is one of the most misunderstood stories in all of Judeo-Christian scripture. This is one of the so-called "clobber" passages, used to condemn homosexuality, and yet a closer reading of the text shows that the sin of Sodom had much more to do with sexual violence and the violation of Hebrew hospitality norms.

Many biblical scholars believe this story was inserted later into the Abrahamic narrative as a divine judicial inquiry for one of the most perplexing questions of the human experience: why do bad things happen to good people? In the text, Abraham and Sarah have set up camp in an oak grove in Mamre, when three travelers come by in the heat of the day. Abraham runs out to meet them, offers them water to drink, and washes their feet; he feeds them bread and cheese and even has a calf butchered for these strangers—a generous act of hospitality and a stark contrast to the reception that these same three visitors receive when they arrive later in Sodom.

When the visitors are preparing to leave, there is a dialogue in which God asks internally if God should hide from Abraham what God is thinking of doing, and ultimately decides to reveal God's plan. God sends the angels into Sodom to see if everything that God has heard about the evil of this city is, in fact, true. And if it is, fire from heaven will be the only recourse.

Sodom is not just any city for Abraham. It is where his brother and his family live. He knows that not everyone in that place is evil. In fact, there are people there for whom he cares deeply. And so Abraham begins to bargain with God, appealing to God's innate characteristic of justice.

This exchange between Abraham and God shows that God is willing to engage with Abraham, to hear his concerns for the people in the city. God cares about what Abraham thinks, and when he calls upon God's fairness and compassion, it's almost as if God wants a reason to spare the city from destruction.

Abraham intercedes with God for a more just and merciful outcome. We still use this word—*intercession*—when we pray. We may, or may not, expect that God will answer our prayers exactly as we have asked them or on our time line, but still, we have the boldness of faith to ask them because we believe in a God who listens to us and our concerns, a God who cares about us and our lives, a God who can be moved to respond.

Bringing the Text to Life

- This sermon could take the shape of a dialogue between Abraham and God.

- Bargaining is considered one of the stages of grief. For a pastoral perspective, consider how Abraham's grief is part of his bargaining with God.

Ideas for Preaching on Luke 11:1-13

There are parallels in this Gospel lesson with the reading from Genesis concerning the obligations and limitations of hospitality. This version of the Lord's Prayer is set within a context of Jesus's teaching about God's generosity and compassion as compared to ours. We can pray to God, asking for what we need for ourselves and for others, because we know that God's giving far outpaces our own.

In verse 8, some versions of the Bible use the word *persistence*, but in the NIV Jesus tells his disciples that because of their "shameless audacity," God will give them whatever they ask for in prayer. Rarely do we think of prayer in such terms, but there are times when we are in such desperate need that our prayers become audacious. Our need to ask something of God is beyond shame because no one but God can provide what we seek. This story, these instructions on prayer, give us permission to lay our souls bare before God, to ask for what our souls need and hope for, and to trust in God's willingness to hear and to respond.

So often we say this prayer that Jesus teaches to his disciples without even really considering how powerful the words are, and what we might really be asking for. When we pray in this pattern, we recognize God's power, mercy, provision for our lives in the most ordinary and extraordinary of ways. In this prayer we are also accepting our dependance on God and our willingness to trust in this relationship with our Heavenly Father/Mother, and to try and live out of God's grace for us in our relationships with others. This is truly an audacious prayer when we take the time to really think about what it is that we are saying.

Bringing the Text to Life

- One way into this story is to talk about the person(s) who taught you to pray? And how did they teach you? How did this instruction help create a foundation of your prayer life?

- Consider offering new and different ways of praying and using prayer stations, breath prayers, or a labyrinth in your worship.

- Use different versions of the Lord's Prayer, or invite worshippers to pray this prayer in different languages.

Notes

August 3, 2025–Eighth Sunday after Pentecost

Hosea 11:1-11; Psalm 107:1-9, 43; Ecclesiastes 1:2, 12-14; 2:18-23; Psalm 49:1-12; Colossians 3:1-11; Luke 12:13-21

Rachel Cornwell

Preacher to Preacher Prayer

Holy One, fill your preachers with an extra measure of compassion and grace as they prepare this week, so that those who feel isolated, broken, and disconnected will find a path home.

Ideas for Preaching on Hosea 11:1-11

Hosea is one of the "minor" prophets of the eighth century BCE, whose ministry took place during the reign of some of Judah's more notable kings—Uzziah, Jotham, Ahaz, and Hezekiah—as well as Israel's king Jeroboam. He prophesied in the era leading up to the fall of Israel to Assyria. The marriage between Hosea and Gomer, and the infidelity in their marriage, is a metaphor describing the relationship between God and Israel.

But this particular passage is not about marriage, but depicts God as a parent who has raised Israel from infancy, teaching them to walk, leading them in paths of faithfulness with "cords of kindness" and "bands of love." Cheek to cheek, God holds this people close, offering them food from God's own hand. Despite the fact that Israel continues to run away, turning to idols and other gods, Yahweh refuses to reject or destroy them. There will be consequences—exile and domination by a foreign power—but God will never stop loving them.

Anyone who has parented a rebellious child, loved a person whose behavior has been hurtful, or stayed in a relationship with someone who has betrayed their trust will be able to identify with the divine pain in this text. This passage may help those who struggle with codependency, loss, and broken relationships to know that God feels their pain. For those who have hurt someone that they love, this passage may allow them to see the harm they have caused and to try to make amends.

Because the feelings and expressions of intimacy in this passage are so relatable, they may reopen wounds or cause feelings of guilt or shame. Preachers need to tread carefully. Relationships are messy. Loving people isn't easy. But when we can acknowledge our hurt and face the consequences of our actions, forgiveness is possible. Even if human relationships are not reconcilable, we can always seek forgiveness from God who will never turn away from us.

Bringing the Text to Life

The ninth step of recovery is to make amends to people we have harmed through our addiction, except when doing so would cause further harm. It takes a lot of work to get to this step in recovery and there are many powerful stories that have been shared publicly about how this step has changed lives. The idea of making amends may be an accessible way of helping us understand our human need to both offer and receive forgiveness.

Ideas for Preaching on Luke 12:13-21

God calls the farmer at the center of this parable a "fool" because in the midst of his prosperity, he does not see how his life is connected to God and to others. This farmer is good at what he does. His fields produce well, so well that his yields are more than he has room to store in his existing barns, and he's wondering what to do with his abundance. He is convinced that the point of life is, actually, to have more than what one needs, so he decides to tear down his barns and build bigger ones so he can hoard his excessive wealth. He's a fool. But he's not the only one.

In our era of unbridled greed, where the chasm between the wealthiest and the poorest continues to widen, we need to hear this message now more than ever. The problem in this parable is not simply that the farmer is greedy. We hear in his self-ruminations that what he really longs for is safety, for security, for happiness. He believes that full barns will allow him to finally "take it easy. Eat, drink, and enjoy [myself]" (v. 19). This is the deep need that underlies his desire to store up his wealth.

But the real reason why he cannot relax, why he doesn't feel satisfied or safe, is because he's disconnected. Disconnected from God and from his neighbor. He has no sense of responsibility to the laborers who helped him till and plant his field, without whom he would not have had such an abundant harvest. He has no humility before God, who gave the growth through good seed, rich soil, sunshine, and abundant rain. He believes that he's self-made and self-sufficient, and all that he has is his alone.

The safety and security that this fool longs for cannot be found in isolation, by cutting himself off from connection and community. It cannot be attained through wealth that is hoarded or security that is limited to only caring about oneself. We are created for relationship with God and with one another, to belong to a community where mutuality, respect, generosity, and love are offered in abundance. The true path to happiness requires us to reject a mentality of scarcity and embrace a spirituality of abundance in which everyone can thrive together.

Bringing the Text to Life

There is no shortage of examples of crass consumerism in our world today, of people who seek happiness, safety, and security through the accumulation of wealth and possessions. The challenge with this parable is not just to point our fingers at those with excessive wealth, but to help all of us to examine how our economic life is set up to create selfishness and disconnection from each other.

Notes

August 10, 2025–Ninth Sunday after Pentecost

Isaiah 1:1, 10-20, Psalm 50:1-8, 22-23; **Genesis 15:1-6**; *Psalm 33:12-22;
Hebrews 11:1-3, 8-16;* **Luke 12:32-40**

Rachel Cornwell

Preacher to Preacher Prayer

Most Glorious God, you have called us ordinary humans to the extraordinary task of proclaiming your good news to the church. Grant us humility and boldness as we respond to this call.

Ideas for Preaching on Genesis 15:1-6

Before Abram became Abraham, before he entered into the covenant with God to become the Father of three of the world's major faith traditions, he was just a man, living an ordinary life in the Mesopotamian village of Ur (modern-day Iraq). He and his wife, Sarai, were in their seventies and childless—well beyond the stage of life when most people started families—when God called them to leave their home and go to a foreign land to fulfill a calling to become the founders of a new nation of God's own people.

Abram heeds this call from God, but he still has some questions about how this plan is going to work, exactly. How can he fulfill the covenant with God when he has no children? His heir- apparent is an enslaved named Eliezer. God doesn't object to Abram's questions but tells him to go outside and look up at the night sky. God then promises that Abram's descendants will be as numerous as the stars.

The story of Abram stands out in scripture because it seems so unique. God may have worked this way in ancient history, calling ordinary people to extraordinary things, but is this how God acts in our modern world? Each one of us is both as humble as earth—from dust you are made and to dust you will return—and we are as glorious and gleaming as the stars in the heavens. Why can't God use you, me, each of us, to fulfill God's purposes, to bring life from places we once thought were barren? God still calls ordinary, everyday people to step out in faith, to go to new places and to be the beginning of something that can change the world.

This is not just a story of Abram and Sarai, but also of Hagar and Eliezer, of Isaac and Ishmael, and of all of us who call ourselves children of Abraham. We are part of God's ongoing story, and God continues to call people to look up, to step out in faith, to leave the comfortable and familiar, and step into something new.

Bringing the Text to Life

There is a Serbian proverb that speaks to the complexity of how humans are made:

Be humble, you are made of earth. Be noble, you are made of stars. This text invites the preacher to consider the ways in which God is still calling ordinary people to do extraordinary things. Who are the people in your community, your congregation who have taken the risk to respond to God's call on their life? How has it changed them and those around them?

Ideas for Preaching on Luke 12:32-40

It was only Labor Day weekend, but the big box store already had Christmas displays up.

Be ready! They seemed to say. *Don't let the holidays sneak up on you, or you may end up with nothing but a tangled string of burned-out lights at the ninth hour!*

It's not just the anticipation of those things that we can easily predict—dates on the calendar that roll around every year—that drives our desire to be prepared. In our post-pandemic world, with a rapidly changing climate, the idea of being prepared has taken on new urgency. Who knows when the next variant or the next major storm will come through and turn life upside down? The need to be ready at an unexpected time is a present and practical reality. Because when we are prepared, we don't need to be afraid. We are ready.

The Gospels were written at a time when the church was still anxiously expecting that Jesus would return, and soon. So, it made sense to be ready, to keep lamps lit, to be dressed and ready for when God would come and fulfill all promises of judgment, justice, and restoration. For a long time, these words of Jesus didn't seem to make a whole lot of sense in our modern world. Things were stable, secure, or so we thought. But now, we understand the idea of urgency, of preparedness, of waiting with expectation a bit better than we did a generation or two ago. The world is changing rapidly all around us, and we need to stay alert.

Fear and change (as well as fear *of* change) have the potential to make us less generous, as we become more anxious about our own security. We might be inclined to build up wealth and dependance on earthly possessions because we don't know what the future will bring. But Jesus invites us instead to hold these things loosely, to share what we have with those who have less than we do. Because we need one another even more when things are uncertain. And we need to trust in God, who has all of us and all of creation held in God's protective care. We may not know the day or the hour, but we know that God is, and always will be, with us.

Bringing the Text to Life

- Consider the upcoming events, occasions, and important dates that are on your church calendar. How is the community getting ready? How does the way in which we prepare for the planned and expected differ for how we plan for those things for which we do not know the day or the hour they will occur?

- What were the lessons that you and your congregation learned about being ready as you came out of the COVID-19 pandemic? How has your approach to being prepared for such unexpected events changed?

Notes

August 17, 2025—Tenth Sunday after Pentecost

Isaiah 5:1-7; *Psalm 80:1-2, 8-19*; *Jeremiah 23:23-29*; *Psalm 82*;
Hebrews 11:29–12:2; *Luke 12:49-56*

Rachel Cornwell

Preacher to Preacher Prayer

God of fruitfulness, we pray that you will bring growth to our people and communities through our preaching this week. Even in places that are chaotic, overgrown or, that feel hopeless to us, we know that you can bring new life. Amen.

Ideas for Preaching on Isaiah 5:1-7

As she walked through her vineyard, Emile Faucheron knew that the grapes were coming too early. In March 2021, there had been record high temperatures in the wine country of Southern France, and the plants were producing well ahead of schedule. Then in one night in April, temperatures dropped quickly, bringing a hard freeze to the region. Vintners lit candles and fires to try and warm their plants. Some even rented helicopters to hover over their vineyards to try and push the warmer air back towards the ground. But as Emilie walked out to her fields the next morning and saw how the fragile buds had frozen and had wilted, she wept. Nearly eighty percent of her crop was destroyed. While wiping away tears, she said, "We put all our passion into it . . . but it's terrible to have spent months working for nothing."[1]

How many of us can relate to this experience, of working passionately on something, giving our heart, labor, sweat, and tears to a project or relationship or job, only to have it destroyed by forces beyond our control?

This prophecy of Isaiah is about the people whom God has lovingly tended and cared for, like a vintner with her vines. It is a love song that God sings for God's people, about the labor God has put in to plant them in rich soil and protect them from external threats. God hoped to see them grow and flourish, but instead of good fruit, the harvest was spoiled and rotten. There was nothing more God could have done. God's only option is to let the vineyard be destroyed and overgrown. The love song has become a lament, over what could have been and what has been lost.

It is God's nature to be a fruit-bearing God, a loving, passionate vine grower who brings life out of death. In the midst of seasons of loss and grief, of pain and destruction, God is yet working to clear away the overgrowth and the thorns and begin again and again and again. In the ecology of God's grace, nothing is ever lost or forsaken.

Bringing the Text to Life

The poem "Backyard" by Mary Oliver[2] speaks to the beauty of nature that is wild and untended, the ways in which places that sometimes look messy and chaotic are actually full of life and the potential for more: "The paths grew damp and uncomfortable and mossy until nobody could get through but a mouse or shadow . . . the birds loved it."

Ideas for Preaching on Hebrews 11:29–12:2

This well-known passage from Hebrews celebrates the remarkable faith of the biblical giants we know so well from Sunday school and VBS. These are the stories of faith that sound like superhero stories: oceans parted, lions' mouths fixed shut, city walls crumbling to rubble, all leading up to Jesus, "the pioneer and perfecter of our faith," who endured the shame and suffering of the cross, but who is now seated at the right hand of God.

But when we read all the verses of this epistle, we also hear about those whose faith did not lead to greatness. For some, their faith led to great suffering. Followers of Jesus were tortured, imprisoned, stoned to death, persecuted, tormented, exiled: "All these people didn't receive what was promised, though they were given approval for their faith" (11:39).

It's one thing to talk about the ways in which great faith has resulted in good things. But what about those whose faith has led them into places of conflict, struggle, and sacrifice, through deep, dark valleys of pain? Or those whose quiet faith has simply held them through daily trials or just the ordinariness of life? Isn't their faith also remarkable and worthy of praise?

Most of the people listening to our sermons are those whose faith looks like a prayer that gets them through another day of work, another day of caregiving. Their faith strengthens them for another round of chemo, another session of therapy, another AA meeting, another week of trying to stretch their paycheck to make ends meet. In and through the lives of these faithful ones is a great cloud of witnesses whose trust in God has sustained them through the daily battles of being human. And their faith ought to be just as inspiring as our biblical heroes.

Bringing the Text to Life

- The litany of the faithful witnesses could be expanded by inviting the congregation to name those whose faith has inspired or sustained them—inviting people to call out names a various points in worship or during the sermon, writing names on paper to be brought to the altar or taped on the walls of your worship space, or putting together photos in a slideshow that plays throughout the sermon.

- At the Tokyo Summer Olympics in 2021, American runner Isaiah Jewett fell in the 800-meter semi-final race, and a runner from Botswana—Nijel Amos—tripped over him. As the two men picked themselves off, they realized that all the other runners had sprinted ahead towards the finish line, so they wrapped their arms around each other's waist and crossed the finish line together. Jewett later said in an interview that he was devastated by what had happened, but "I learned from all the superhero animations I watch, regardless of how mad you are, you have to be a hero at the end of the day. [By] standing up and showing good character, [heroes] show their humanity through who they are."[3]

Notes

August 24, 2025–Eleventh Sunday after Pentecost

Jeremiah 1:4-10; Psalm 71:1-6; Isaiah 58:9b-14; Psalm 103:1-8;
Hebrews 12:18-29; **Luke 13:10-17**

Rachel Cornwell

Preacher to Preacher Prayer

God, touch our lips and give us the words for another week. Help us speak the truth in love. Remind us that no matter how people respond, you know us inside and out and your grace will always be enough.

Ideas for Preaching on Jeremiah 1:4-10

Tradition teaches that Jeremiah authored the books of Kings and Lamentations, as well as the prophetic book that bears his name. From the thirteenth year of Josiah's reign until the fall of Jerusalem and the destruction of the temple in 587 BCE, Jeremiah's ministry spanned the reign of five kings and a time of great turmoil in Judah. It is for this reason that he is sometimes called "the weeping prophet," because the words of truth he was called to speak to God's people in those challenging times broke his heart. His preaching resulted in his rejection and persecution as he prophesied the great suffering that would come to the kingdom of Judah.

The book of Jeremiah takes us all the way back to his call as a child. The son of a priest, Jeremiah (like most preacher's kids) knew what was involved in the job he was being called to. Unlike another prophet, Isaiah, who cried out, "Here I am! Send me!" Jeremiah did not feel worthy, prepared, or equipped for the task God was calling him to do. "I'm just a boy," Jeremiah responded.

But we hear God affirm Jeremiah's calling, telling him that before he was knit together in his mother's womb, God already knew him, knew what his life's purpose was going to be. What a powerful affirmation, to be known so intimately by God, to hear that Jeremiah's calling was so deeply a part of him that it was in his very blood and bones.

To feel inadequate, insecure, or unprepared for a difficult task is so very relatable. Even if we are afraid to admit it, every person knows this feeling. And yet, how empowering might it be to imagine God speaking to each of us, saying: "I know who you are, and what I created you to do. Do not be afraid." Perhaps especially when we know that the work before us is something that will break our hearts, we need the assurance that God will give us what we need to do that which we are called to do.

Bringing the Text to Life

- A servant leader is one who has humility about the work before them and gathers their strength from their relationship with God. This is a powerful text to use to talk about leadership and about the qualities of one who is willing to be faithful, even when it comes at great risk and with great sacrifice.

- The words God speaks about knitting us together in our mother's womb are also found in Psalm 139:13-14. These words would be a powerful refrain throughout a sermon that affirms the sacred worth of all people and our intimate relationship with the Creator God.

Ideas for Preaching on Luke 13:10-17

Most of us are familiar with Sabbath, at least as an idea, if not a regular practice. There are those of us who may have grown up at a time or place where Sabbath-keeping was more ingrained in the culture; where businesses closed on Sundays and there was not much to do but go to church. Many people who grew up in this way do not remember the Sabbath as a gift, but rather as an oppressive obligation, a restriction on all the fun things that they really wanted to do. Like so many good things, religion can often take something that was designed as a gift from God and make it feel like a rule that had to be followed.

In this healing story, the leader of the synagogue reacts to Jesus's healing on the Sabbath with righteous indignation because Jesus had the audacity to break the rules. The rules had been created to give structure and order to people's lives, to help them stay in relationship with God, to remind them of their relationship with God. But sometimes when we are in a position of power and authority, when it's our responsibility to enforce the rules, we can forget the reason why they are there in the first place.

When we try to see this interaction from the perspective of this religious leader, we can maybe see that he had a point. After all, there were six other days of the week when Jesus could have done this healing. This poor woman had been suffering for eighteen long years. Could Jesus not have waited one more day to perform his miracle?

Luke describes the synagogue leader and those who support following the rules as Jesus's opponents. The text says that Jesus puts them to shame. But surely Jesus had compassion for them too. Jesus must have seen the ways in which the covenant had become a burden for them; that their backs were so bowed with the weight of enforcing rules, they couldn't "[rejoice] at all the extraordinary things" Jesus was doing right before their eyes (v. 17).

Bringing the Text to Life

- This story of Jesus and his "opponents" is so relatable in our polarized culture, where we are so tempted to view anyone different from us as a threat. How can this Gospel help speak to the temptation to call those who may disagree with us "opponents" and instead see them as people who are also worthy of receiving the delight and wonder of Christ's love?

- Where are the places in your context where the religious rules are exclusive or limiting, privileged over people's liberation? What would it take to change them?

Notes

August 31, 2025–Twelfth Sunday after Pentecost

Jeremiah 2:4-13; Psalm 81:1, 10-16; Sirach 10:12-18 or Proverbs 25:6-7; Psalm 112; **Hebrews 13:1-8, 15-16; Luke 14:1, 7-14**

Rachel Cornwell

Preacher to Preacher Prayer

Gracious God, rank us with whom you will. As we prepare our sermons this week, help us to remember that you do not care about rank or social status. But call us to treat all people as our siblings in Christ.

Ideas for Preaching on Hebrews 13:1-8, 15-16

Every morning when my kids leave for school, my spouse sends them forth with the same benediction. "Make a good day!" he says. And what he means is that out there in the world, things are going to happen which will be frustrating, disappointing, and mostly out of your control. You may not have a good day, but if you can keep a good attitude and perspective, you can still make a good day.

The dense and theologically rich letter is full of instructions written to some followers of Jesus who are starting to doubt whether Jesus actually is the Messiah they have been waiting for. Throughout the letter, the author tells their audience to hold fast, to fix their thoughts on Jesus, and to be careful not to drift away. The author strives to connect the Hebrews' messianic hope with the life, death, and resurrection of Jesus throughout this letter. These are the words of someone who has been there, who has also struggled with the same questions, doubts, and worries and wants to encourage these fellow believers to keep the faith. And when we get to chapter 13, the letter concludes with a series of exhortations on how to live in a way that keeps their faith alive, not just for them, but as a witness to the wider world.

The Christian community at this time was facing great challenges such as persecution, schism and divisions, as well as losing people who had given up and drifted away. The struggles of the first-century church are not unlike the struggles of the twenty-first-century church in this way. Which means these exhortations are for us as well.

In the end, this is what it means to be a follower of Jesus: *Love one another. Be in solidarity with those who are suffering. Show hospitality to strangers. Honor your covenant relationships. Don't be greedy. Be inspired by those whose faith you admire and try to live like they do.* There is much in the world that you can't control, but if we commit ourselves to this way of faith, we will stay in love with God and show others what it means to be one of Christ's disciples.

Bringing the Text to Life

A person's last words can sometimes tell us a lot about their life. Reggae singer Bob Marley's last words were: "Money can't buy life." Singer Whitney Houston said, "I'm going to go and see Jesus." And for the "quiet" Beatle, George Harrison's last words when he finally succumbed to lung cancer in 2001 were, "Love one another."

Ideas for Preaching on Luke 14:1, 7-14

Luke tells us a story from Jesus's life when he was invited to the home of a respected religious leader for a meal on the Sabbath. The text says that the Pharisees were all watching him; after all, he would have been considered an honored guest. Everyone would have wanted to see where he was going to sit.

But Jesus stands on the outside edge of the room, watching as people are searching out their seats for the meal, jockeying for a position of privilege. This scene is reminiscent of a middle school cafeteria, where the "cool kids" are all sitting together, while the nerds, the loners, and the social outcasts sit elsewhere.

Instead of sitting down, Jesus turns to his disciples and offers them advice for two different scenarios. First, he says, if you are invited to a dinner, find the lowest seat. That way you won't be embarrassed if someone more important tells you to move. But if you are invited to move up, you will be recognized for your humility. But if you are hosting, don't invite your friends or relatives or wealthy neighbors, but instead be sure that your guests are from among those who are considered the lowest in society. That way they can't pay you back. But you will receive your reward at the resurrection of the righteous.

It seems that Jesus isn't just saying this for the sake of his disciples, but he's speaking loud enough that everyone in the room can hear what he's saying. He's not just talking about some future event, a hypothetical dinner party that they might be invited to in the future. Jesus is critiquing the status-seeking behavior of his host and everyone in the room.

The lectionary omits verses 2-6, in which the first thing Jesus does is to challenge his host and his friends, asking them if the law allows for healing to take place on the Sabbath. Then he cures a sick man in their presence, leaving them speechless. The lectionary likely omits these verses because they are so similar to last week's Gospel lesson. But they add to the growing tension between Jesus and the religious establishment and show that Jesus's focus is on challenging the systems and behaviors that create hierarchies among people, which privilege status over compassion and rules over righteousness.

Bringing the Text to Life

According to etiquette expert Emily Post, "When entertaining dignitaries . . . the host or hostess of an official luncheon or dinner seats the guests according to rank. Guests who have no protocol ranking are seated according to the unspoken rank the host assigns to them. The host ranks guests as he chooses, basing his decision on age, social prominence, personal accomplishments, and mutual interests shared by seatmates."[4]

Notes

September 7, 2025– Thirteenth Sunday after Pentecost

Jeremiah 18:1-11; ***Deuteronomy 30:15-20****; Philemon 1:1-21;*
Luke 14:25-33

Charley Reeb

Preacher to Preacher Prayer

Eternal God, sometimes you call us to challenge listeners and speak hard truths. Give us the courage to be prophets for you. Lord, while we prepare this week's message remind us of our own sins and shortcomings so that the word we share will be genuine and come from a place of love and understanding. Amen.

Ideas for Preaching on Deuteronomy 30:15-20

This passage in Deuteronomy is a small section of Moses' last speech to the Israelites before they entered the Promised Land. Moses led God's people out of Egypt and back to the land that God gave to their forefathers. After 40 years in the desert, the time had come for God's people to cross the Jordan River and enter the land God has promised them. Because Moses knew he could not go with them he gave them one last bit of wisdom. Much of what Moses said to the Israelites was simply a warning not to repeat the same mistakes they had made in the wilderness. Moses knew that as they entered the land filled with milk and honey the temptation to disobey God would be even greater. Being comfortable often leads to complacency and complacency is not always a friend to wise and healthy decisions. In this passage, Moses was urging his people to stay vigilant. Keep God's commandments and put God first. The choice was clear: "See, I have set before you today life and good, death and evil... choose life" (30:15, 19).

Bringing the Text to Life

- Since this text is assigned at the beginning of September, the start of a new a school year, take advantage of Moses' words of wisdom. Speak to the students in your church about making good choices ("choose life"). Also be sure to speak to the parents about making good choices too! Encourage them to set an example for their kids by making their faith a priority. Summer vacations are over and it is time to get back to attending worship and Bible study on a regular basis.

- Think of ways you could illustrate the contrast between choosing life or choosing death. What images could you put on the screen that demonstrate life and death? A memorable picture could make a significant impact. For example, I know a preacher who showed a picture of "Dante's View" in Death Valley. From Dante's view you can see Black Water, a depression in the earth two hundred feet below sea level. It is the lowest point in the United States. But from Dante's view you can also see the highest peak in the United States–Mt. Whitney.

- Moses's words remind us that some decisions in life are "crossroad decisions." Give examples of such decisions—who we choose to marry; how we choose to respond when tempted to compromise our values; what we choose to do about our health when we are confronted with a sobering report from the doctor. Will we "choose life" or "death"?

- What are some of the modern-day idols we are tempted to put before God?

Ideas for Preaching on Luke 14:25-33

The heading for this passage in Luke reads "The Cost of Being a Disciple." You could also use this heading: "How Not to Grow a Church." This text isn't exactly a seminar on how to attract a crowd for Sunday morning worship. If you are looking for church growth tips from Jesus, you will be disappointed. In fact, the text implies that it was a large crowd which prompted Jesus to say these words. He didn't want people to be misled about what it meant to follow him. If we took today's text seriously, we would have ushers and greeters greeting new people at the sanctuary door, not with a bulletin, but with a clipboard showing a list of questions:

"Are you absolutely sure you want to follow this way of life?"

"Are you absolutely sure you are willing to give Jesus everything you have?"

"Are you absolutely sure you are willing to put aside everything that matters to you for the sake of the gospel, even family?"

"If you are not, you may want to go home and think this over. This is not a country club you're joining."

This is a challenging text. How should a preacher handle it? There is no way to soften these words. There is a cost to following Jesus. One way to approach this passage for a sermon is to explain how it is a warning: following Jesus will change you. Jesus will turn your life upside down and rearrange your priorities. Jesus' comment about "hating" family is a bit disturbing but Jesus wasn't calling us to hate in the way we think of that word. He was talking about priorities. If you are following Jesus, don't be surprised if you begin putting him above your family. This text gives the requirements for following Jesus but it also explains the consequences of following him. Jesus is not interested in growing churches. He wants to grow disciples. An inductive sermon form could be an effective way to preach this text.

Bringing the Text to Life

- I remember a man approaching me after a worship service and saying, "I didn't like your sermon today. In fact, I don't like a lot of your sermons."

  "Oh really?" I replied. "Well, thanks for your honesty. Why is that? Do tell."

  "Well, your sermons make me feel uncomfortable. I don't come to church for that. I come to church for some peace and comfort."

  I responded, "Well, you picked the wrong faith. I didn't have problems until I met Jesus."

- Give examples in your sermon of how this text is often in conflict with the way the church and culture portray Jesus and what it looks like to follow him.

- Offer true stories of people you know who "carry their cross"—sacrifice their desires and priorities for the sake of following Jesus.

- Explain the role Wesley's understanding of sanctifying grace plays in being a disciple. Be sure to mention that living out this text in Luke is about being perfected in love. Our love for Jesus and others is what motivates and empowers us to carry our cross. Our sacrifices are, in fact, acts of love and point to Jesus' ultimate demonstration of love on the cross.

Notes

September 14, 2025– Fourteenth Sunday after Pentecost

*Jeremiah 4:11-12, 22-28; Exodus 32:7-17; **1 Timothy 1:12-17;** **Luke 15:1-10***

Charley Reeb

Preacher to Preacher Prayer

Lord, you have given us the privilege and responsibility of preparing and preaching your word. Please make us equal to this sacred task. Give us the words to speak so that listeners will not hear our voice but your voice. We surrender ourselves so that we may be your vessels of love and grace. Amen.

Ideas for Preaching on 1 Timothy 1:12-17

Paul's words in this text should help us preachers remember to speak plainly in our sermons. Paul doesn't get highly theological in this passage. He is direct about his sinfulness and how Jesus has "saved" him. One way to preach this text is to reinforce the idea the Jesus came to "seek and save the lost" (something that will tie in well with the gospel lesson). Our congregations need to be reminded that one of the church's main roles is to be a vessel of God's saving love and grace in Jesus Christ. We are called to preach Jesus as the help and hope of the world. This sounds obvious enough but churches and preachers can lose sight of proclaiming the gospel. Sharing the good news is what sets us apart from non-profits and secular charities. Unless we are lifting up Jesus as the Savior of the world, why should the world see us as any different than Rotary or Kiwanis? After all, many nonprofits feed the hungry, serve the poor and gather regularly to recite creeds. What makes the church different is that we are God's chosen vessel empowered by the Holy Spirit to share the good news of Jesus Christ.

Bringing the Text to Life

- List the similarities between churches and nonprofits and then share what makes the church different.

- If you are bold, mention how many professions of faith your church has recorded in the last five years. This will put things into perspective. Invite your congregation to invite others to church and to respectfully share their faith with co-workers, friends and loved ones.

- Consider sharing your own testimony about how Jesus saved you.

- If you are planning a stewardship series for September, this is a useful text to remind your people why it is important to give to the church. The church is not just another charity. The church is the body of Christ that is charged with the task of sharing the saving love and grace of Christ. The church needs money and resources in order to accomplish its mission.

Ideas for Preaching on Luke 15:1-10

If you have chosen to preach on this text, you may be concerned about finding something to say that has not already been said. While not an original approach, consider focusing your sermon on what prompted Jesus to share these well known parables in the first place—his association with "tax collectors and sinners." The irony is that even though Luke 15 is a very familiar text, many Christians act as if they have never read it. A sermon on this text could address modern day pharisaical attitudes. For example, how often do we hear this excuse from someone who does not attend worship: "The church is filled with a bunch of hypocrites." These verses in Luke 15 remind us that, of course, the church is filled with a bunch of hypocrites. Isn't that where lost and sinful people should be? You don't need a bath if you're clean. If everyone were perfect, we would not need Jesus or the church?

The attitude conveyed by the Pharisees in this text is also an all too familiar one inside the church. Examples of judgmental remarks and looks from churchgoers are too numerous to mention. It never occurs to those passing judgment that by doing so they have become hypocrites themselves. The so called "unsavory" person in the pew that is looked down upon may just sin differently than some of us. We are all sinners in desperate need of a Savior. The truth is the Pharisees mentioned in this text are just as lost as that sheep that needs to be found.

If we are honest, each of us have played all the roles in this passage. We have been lost in our sin. We have been lost in our judgements. In our better moments, we have been the one looking for the lost or waiting expectantly for the lost to be found because we know what it is like to be lost. The good news is that we have a relentless Savior who will stop at nothing to bring all of us home.

Bringing the Text to Life

- Mention a time you lost something valuable and the joy you experienced in finding it.

- Share an example of when you acted like the Pharisees in this text and how you were corrected.

- Compare the Pharisees in the text to the elder son in the parable of the prodigal son later in the chapter. Jesus was clever in not sharing whether or not the elder son joined the party for the younger brother. We must decide for ourselves if we will join the party for the one who was lost but now is found.

- Research and share why so many people are turned off by Christians and have no desire to attend church. Studies have shown that a prominent reason why younger generations don't attend church is because of the judgmental attitudes of Christians. Hypocrisy among Christians is also mentioned, which is an ironically prophetic word from those who are apparently "lost."

Notes

September 21–Fifteenth Sunday after Pentecost

*Jeremiah 8:18-9:1; **Amos 8:4-7; 1 Timothy 2:1-7**; Luke 16:1-13*

Charley Reeb

Preacher to Preacher Prayer

Lord, you have called us to proclaim the truth of the gospel. Give us the courage to preach boldly and with conviction. Fill our cup Lord, so that we may pour into listeners the life giving and transforming message of your good news for all people. Amen.

Ideas for Preaching on Amos 8:4-7

This is a powerfully prophetic word from the minor prophet on greed and cheating the poor. Amos tells us that God does not forget those who have mistreated the poor and oppressed. This text and many others in the Bible make it clear that God has a heart for the needy and marginalized. This passage in Amos gives the preacher an opportunity to focus on social justice and how we are called to serve the poor and speak truth to power.

Bringing the Text to Life

- Explain John Wesley's understanding of social holiness and how growing closer to Christ draws us closer to the poor, oppressed and marginalized. Mention that Wesley practiced what he preached by vehemently opposing slavery, serving the poor, and investing in medical care and education.

- Reference other passages in the Old Testament that call for justice for the oppressed and service to the poor and destitute.

- Make a connection between this text and the parable of the sheep and goats found in Matthew 25 where we find that when we serve those in need we are also serving Jesus. This is how intimately connected Jesus is with those who suffer.

- Give a call to action for the congregation to serve in a ministry or mission of the church that provides for the poor and hungry. Offer testimony of how your church reaches out to help the needy. Give concrete examples and tell a story about someone who has been helped by the ministries of your church.

- Give current examples of greed and mistreatment of the poor mentioned in the text. In what ways do the powers that be neglect and mistreat people, especially the poor? How can the church respond and work to change our oppressive systems?

Ideas for Preaching on 1 Timothy 2:1-7

The Apostle Paul covers a lot of ground in these seven verses. He calls us to pray for those in authority so that we may live in peace. He quickly shifts into expressing how God wants everyone to hear the truth of the gospel and be saved. He then underscores the message of the gospel—that Jesus gave his life as a ransom for all people. Lastly, Paul reminds his readers of his authority and that God called him to be an apostle. He even feels compelled to mention that he is not lying. This is not the only place in the New Testament where we see Paul defending himself as an apostle. It is clear that Paul's authority was often questioned by some people in the church.

There is enough in this text to write several sermons but it is clear that the dominant theme is the message of the gospel. It would be helpful and useful to break down the gospel we have been called to proclaim. Preachers often make the mistake of assuming that listeners already know and understand the gospel but that is simply not the case. This text provides the opportunity to clearly explain the eternal and life transforming significance of the birth, life, teachings, death and resurrection of Jesus.

A powerful focal point for a sermon on this text would be the word "ransom." This is the same word Jesus himself used to explain his redemptive work on the cross (Mark 10:45; Matthew 20:28). Many think that the word "ransom" refers to penal substitutionary atonement—that Jesus paid the penalty or price of our sins. We deserved the punishment but God sent Jesus to take our place. However, there is perhaps a different way of understanding the concept of ransom. Ransoms are not demanded by good people. They are demanded by bad people—kidnappers or other criminals. Therefore, another way of understanding the atonement is that Jesus paid the devil's ransom for us. Evil sought to destroy humanity but Jesus took the devil's bullet for us and paid the price the devil desired for humanity. This understanding of the cross could be liberating for many listeners who struggle with penal substitutionary atonement.

Bringing the Text to Life

- Explain how there are different ways of understanding the atonement—Christus Victor, Moral Theory, "Ransom", etc.

- Describe your faith journey as it relates to the atonement. Which perspective speaks most to you?

- Create a study guide for small groups to discuss your sermon and the idea of the atonement.

- Give an altar call and offer the invitation to receive Christ as Lord and Savior. If an altar call doesn't fit the culture of your church, ask listeners to pray silently after you as you offer a prayer of confession, repentance and surrender to Christ. Give them the option of reaching out to you if they made a commitment to Christ.

Notes

September 28–Sixteenth Sunday after Pentecost

Jeremiah 32:1-3a, 6-15; Amos 6:1a, 4-7; **1 Timothy 6:6-19;**
Luke 16:19-31

Charley Reeb

Preacher to Preacher Prayer

Eternal God, I desire to be faithful to your call on my life. Guide me as I prepare this sermon and empower me to preach it. Save me from the distractions that would prevent me from giving my best to you in the study and in the pulpit. Lord, make me equal to the task you have set before me. Amen.

Ideas for Preaching on 1 Timothy 6:6-19

This is a rich passage of scripture that contains Paul's warning to young Timothy about the pitfalls that await those who are driven by their love of money. Paul is quick to tell Timothy that greed has ruined many people, especially those who seek to follow Christ. The seductive lure of wealth and how it can change people is an old story but one that bears repeating. When preaching on this text it is important to mention that Paul is not condemning those who are rich. Being rich is not the problem. In fact, the generosity of the wealthy has equipped many a church to live out its mission of making disciples of Jesus Christ. It's what we do with our money and our attitude about it that determines its influence. Churches need money to fund ministry, compensate staff, and maintain facilities. Without money and the people who are generous with it, the church could not be the church. If we use money as a tool by which the church accomplishes its mission then money can bring many blessings. However, problems arise when people forget the rightful place of money and turn it into an idol. Paul reminds us that it is the *love* of money that is the source of all sorts of evil.

Verses 17-19 give us three key preaching ideas:

1. Money is fleeting so there is no hope in it (v. 17)

2. We are commanded to generously share our resources (v. 18)

3. Our giving has eternal significance (v. 19)

Bringing the Text to Life

- Consider using this passage or portions of it as the guiding text for an annual stewardship campaign. There are many phrases that could be used as the seed of your campaign theme or message. For example, "rich in good deeds"; "take hold of the life that is truly life"; "fight the good fight of the faith."

- Make the connection between the message of this passage and Jesus' parable of the rich fool in Luke 12:13-21. How do the two passages inform one another?

- Since a sermon on this text will be about having the right perspective on money and the importance of being generous with it, ask your congregation to consider the church in their wills and estate planning (v. 7).

Ideas for Preaching on Luke 16:19-21

The story of the Rich Man and Lazarus is a poignant tale. Although a story, its lessons are very real and should give us pause. One clear lesson from the story is that there will be a day of reckoning when the inequities of life will be fixed. Just as Lazarus was comforted in eternity and the rich man was punished for his lack of compassion and generosity, so too we will find the sinful disparity between the rich and poor on earth receiving the judgment of God in heaven. The Bible is replete with warnings to those who ignore the needs of the poor and helpless. It is curious that those Christians who are so quick to talk about sin and the judgment of God seem to ignore the many places in scripture where God commands that we take care of the poor and destitute (Deuteronomy 15:7-11, 26:12; Isaiah 58:7, 10; Matthew 5:42, 19:21; Luke 3:11).

Another lesson we find in this story is that it was what the rich man did not do that condemned him. On earth he simply did not pay attention to the needs of the poor and did nothing to help them. He did not notice the suffering of those in need. This is the very definition of insensitivity. The rich man accepted the plight of the poor as "the way things are" and felt no obligation to alleviate their pain. This attitude pervades our world. So many accept the suffering of the needy as simply a part of life. "He was dealt a bad hand. Some people are just unlucky." Others explain away their lack of sensitivity by claiming, "If they worked hard like me, their lives could change," oblivious to the many advantages and opportunities they receive that the poor do not.

A sermon on this story should be convicting and lead to action by those who have ears to hear.

Bringing the Text to Life

It is easy to see the similarities between this parable and Dickens' *A Christmas Carol*. Mentioning those similarities in a sermon might be useful for your listeners.

Include an invitation in your sermon for people to contribute and volunteer to your church's food pantry and other similar ministries. You may also wish to ask for more donations for your financial assistance fund.

As part of a small group discussion on the sermon, consider asking these questions:

1. In addition to food and shelter, what are some other needs of the poor in our community? Is there a way we can help provide education for the poor and job skills training?

2. How can we make our church facilities more accessible to the poor?

3. How can we provide financial resources for the poor in times of crisis?

Notes

October 5, 2025–
Seventeenth Sunday after
Pentecost

*Lamentations 1:1-6; 3:19-26; Psalm 137; 2 Timothy 1:1-14;
Luke 17:5-10*

Charley Reeb

Preacher to Preacher Prayer

Lord, enable this week's sermon to remind people of your faithfulness. May my words glorify you and express the power of your steadfast love. Give me the wisdom to speak words that instill faith in the hearts of those who have been disappointed. Amen.

Ideas for Preaching on Lamentations 3:19-26

If B.B. King had written a book of the Bible it would have been Lamentations. It contains five poems of cries, regrets and pain. It is filled with "the blues." But unlike most blues songs Lamentations does not express heartache over some bad luck or lost lover. Lamentations expresses the heart-breaking aftermath of Jerusalem being destroyed by evil Babylon. Jeremiah wrote these poems and you can feel his pain as he cries out to God. His agony is tangible as he expresses his grief over the loss of his homeland. The special places he grew up with were destroyed. Many of his friends had been killed. Everything he knew and loved had been wiped out. *"Remember my affliction and my wanderings, the wormwood and the gall! My soul continually remembers it and is bowed down within me"* (v. 19-20).

When preaching on this text it would be a good idea to recognize the genuine pain that is expressed by the biblical writer. It is liberating for people to know that such honest anguish is found in scripture. Too often the Bible is portrayed as a sterile book that is out of touch with the difficulties of life. Passages such as this one remind us how in touch the Bible is with our humanity.

In verses 21-24 we find that even in the midst of his agony Jeremiah still has hope because he remembers the faithfulness of God. Jeremiah is demonstrating for us the powerful spiritual practice of remembering, which is worth noting in a sermon on this text. Too often our pain makes us forget how God has sustained us in past troubles and redeemed our suffering. Jeremiah does not forget to "call to mind" how God has helped him before. This brings him hope for the future.

Jeremiah also has the wisdom and experience not only to ask God for help but to wait patiently for that help to come (v. 25-26). We all have the tendency to ask God for help and quickly move on to what we think is best. Instead, we must wait expectantly for God with open minds and hearts.

Bringing the Text to Life

- Encourage your congregation to keep a prayer journal or diary. This practice helps us remember the faithfulness of God in our lives.

- Include Proverbs 3:5-6 in your sermon, especially as it relates to verses 25 and 26 when Jeremiah speaks of asking God for help. Explain how these wise words from Proverbs help clarify what it means to wait quietly for God.

- Reference other passages of scripture that reflect the act of remembering God's help in the past (Psalm 77:19).

Ideas for Preaching on Luke 17:5-10

Most scholars agree that the first ten verses of Luke 17 make up four distinct and unrelated sections of scripture. Verses 5-10 from this week's text contain sections three (v. 5-6) and four (v. 7-10). Therefore, the best option for the preacher is to pick one of these two sections rather than trying to preach a unified message on the entire passage.

Verses 5 and 6 emphasize the power of faith. It is curious how Jesus responds to the disciples' request for more faith. He tells them how much they could accomplish with a very small amount of faith. The implication is that the disciples need only to use the faith they already have. It is easy for some to scoff at Jesus' remarks especially when considering that over the years many hope hustlers have used Jesus's words to manipulate people. However, we should not allow these unfortunate examples to overshadow the significance of Jesus' message on faith. Once it is understood that faith is simply being willing to rely on God to accomplish his will then the power of faith will emerge. These verses convict us and provoke us to ask ourselves the question: "When was the last time I was trying to accomplish something so significant for God that I had to rely on my faith?" A sermon on these verses of faith would be bolstered by referencing Hebrews 11 and all the achievements from the heroes of faith.

Bringing the Text to Life

So often people misunderstand these verses by thinking, "I can accomplish great things with just a little faith." No, it is God who is doing the heavy lifting! We are simply making ourselves available to God. We often believe our faith and God's power is a 50/50 equation. It's not. It is really 10% us and 90% God.

We get in trouble when we seek to control. Our strength is depleted when we try to orchestrate everything, instead of relying on God for his guidance and power. When everything feels like we are swimming upstream, it is usually because we have not put God in charge. Quite often our pride, fear or stubbornness impede the movement of God in our lives.

Notes

October 12, 2025– Eighteenth Sunday after Pentecost

Jeremiah 29:1, 4-7; *Psalm 66:1-12; 2 Timothy 2:8-15;* ***Luke 17:11-19***

Sarah B. Miller

Preacher to Preacher Prayer

Speak, Lord, your servant is listening. Speak what is true. Amen.

Ideas for Preaching on Jeremiah 29:1, 4-7

This text is a portion of correspondence between the prophet Jeremiah and God's people exiled in Babylon. Jeremiah's words are both prescriptive and descriptive for how God's people ought to be employed during this season.

It is worth noting what is going on behind this text and what has proceeded from this text. World powers of the time wanted possession of the valuable and coveted ports in the promised land. This is one reason for the constant wars during this time; the cause was not just a difference over divinity but also ownership of geography. People then and now rationalize this reality through theology, and depending on the points emphasized, interpretations can be more helpful or more harmful.

God's people received the Decalogue beneath Sinai's heights. As a binding legal document, the Decalogue contained the terms of blessing for obedience to the Law and cursing for disobedience to the Law. God's people knew the commands; even so, for generations, the people acted according to their own desires (Deuteronomy 12:8). God sent priests, judges, and prophets. God gave chances. God was consistent and transparent about the consequences.

In Babylon, God's people also learned the heart lesson that our God is a grace-filled God. While exile may be conceived as a time without creature comforts, it is also a time to center on that which truly comforts the creature. That which truly comforts us connects us with God and neighbor.

Bringing the Text to Life

In moving from text to sermon this week, consider how you will affirm God's steadfast presence in the devasting moments. Consider how and what you will identify as the tools and resources God provides so that good can redeem hardship.

Jeremiah 29 introduces a new set of instruction and terms in which God's people will live and move and have their being (Acts 17:28). To a people who languished on the shores of Babylon's rivers, wept for home, and achingly wondered how they could sing the Lord God's songs in a strange land, the prophet's words would have startled and surprised (Psalm 137:1, 4). "Build. Plant. Marry. Multiply. Seek the welfare of the city." In other words, "get acclimated and get to work as a sign of your restoration of faithfulness to the One True God."

Our God is a startling and surprising God. As soon as we think we have God figured out, God does a new thing such as like instructing God's people, that until this day have lived cloistered lives, to enter the complexity of a polytheistic and pluralistic society and to thrive as neighbors. This is the kind of rule our God desires and is establishing with us, and sometimes in spite of us. When we come alongside God in this work, we make true, physical, and visible God's transformation—for us and for our creation—in real time. Our God is consistent and hopeful throughout our redemption process. In believing we can do the hard things and the heart things, we are able to thrive in relationship with God and neighbor even in strange lands.

Ideas for Preaching on Luke 17:11-19

This passage has two identifiable portions: a healing portion and a salvation portion. The opening verses follow the classic three-fold pattern of healing stories in Scripture: (1) a cry for help; (2) the Divine response; and (3) healing during an act of obedience.

Characteristic of the Third Gospel, salvation comes to a person on the margin or, more appropriately, on the boundary. The phrase in Greek translated to "made well" can also be translated as "to be saved" both presently and eternally.[1] In this text geography is theology. While Jesus is at a physical boundary between Samaria and Galilee, he crosses theological and cultural boundaries, incarnating what it means to be a neighbor, to love neighbor as yourself, to love our enemy, and to include rather than exclude.

The salvation occasion occurs "on the way to Jerusalem" (v. 11). In crying out to Jesus, the ten lepers communicated their dream of deliverance and their belief that Jesus was capable to fulfill it. Generally, lepers were destitute. They were isolated in order to confine contagion and reduce communicable exposure that would render others unclean under the Levitical Holiness Code. Dreams may have been among the few comforts lepers retained. W. B. Yeats concluded his poem "Aedh Wishes for the Clothes of Heaven" with these stanzas:

But I, being poor, have only my dreams;

I have spread my dreams under your feet;

Tread softly because you tread on my dreams.

On his way to Jerusalem, Jesus treads softly. He moves forward mindfully, aware of his power and its potential impact on people's dreams.

Within a mixed economy of people, Jesus names the mixed economy of people healed. Rhetorically and profoundly, Jesus asks, "Weren't ten cleansed? Where are the other nine? No one returned to praise God except this foreigner?" (vv. 17-18). His own countryfolk did not return to offer gratitude; only the one set apart by country, culture, and custom. Having been in contact with Jesus's grace, the Samaritan is not only made clean but also whole, and is newly set apart to "get up and go" to share in gratitude of his healing by Jesus the Savior who would not stand for this or any other boundary further segregating him from life.

Bringing the Text to Life

In moving from text to sermon this week, consider the following:

- At times we find affinity and community through infirmity. Infirmities have ways of drawing unlikely people into community. How does this experience sensitize us? With Christ's help, how can we nurture these relationships beyond the surface experience towards the salvation experience?

- The Samaritan's healing and salvation were miraculous; what stories would be told! What stories would you tell in sharing your faith after having experienced Jesus's healing and salvation?

- Jesus crossed a boundary towards the lepers, especially the Samaritan leper. Likewise, the Samarian leper crossed a boundary towards Jesus. What cultural, societal, and spiritual boundaries keep us and our neighbors from connecting with Christ, which keeps us from complete health and wholeness? What discernments and actions ought to commence in order to dismantle them?

Notes

October 19, 2025– Nineteenth Sunday after Pentecost

Jeremiah 31:27-34; *Psalm 119:97-104; Genesis 32:22-31; Psalm 121;*
2 Timothy 3:14-4:5; **Luke 18:1-8**

Sarah B. Miller

Preacher to Preacher Prayer

Speak, Lord, your servant is listening. Speak what is true. Amen.

Ideas for Preaching on Jeremiah 31:27-34

God's New Covenant will be inscribed on the people's hearts and will deliver them from transgenerational suffering and shame (v. 33). Under the terms of the Decalogue, sins are inheritable; children to the third and fourth generation would suffer punishment for the sins of the first generation (Exodus 20:5). With God's new covenant, no longer so (vv. 29-30)! Writes biblical scholar Walter Brueggemann, "Each new generation can act out its own destiny and choose its own future with God," beginning in and continuing after exile.[2]

Participating in God's restorative work draws us into God's ongoing process and promise of change that is both already underway and awaiting final consummation. We are like *cater flies*— no longer caterpillars and not quite yet butterflies. We are mid-metamorphosis. It is a tender, vulnerable place to be. We can lunge forward or sway back. It is a place packed with potential, and God desires this change in us and for us in order to draw us nearer to God's heart, desires, and preferred future.

Without change, we do not progress. Without change, we will get what we have always got because we will continue to do what we have always done. Changing is courageous work that welcomes us into the world of God's passions and possibilities. Our changing is necessary because while we are people capable of plucking up, breaking down, overthrowing, destroying, and bringing evil, God wants our focus to be building and planting. God wants our focus on and engagement in renewal and restoration. These are both the work and the fruit of salvation, written by God upon our hearts and lived for God throughout our lives.

Bringing the Text to Life

In moving from text to sermon this week, consider the following:

- What transgenerational suffering and shame are present in your congregation, and how has its presence shape—and is still shaping —the congregation. Select a liturgical experience—such as a prayer of confession/words of assurance, litany of silence and response, remembrance of baptism, and/or act of reconciliation—that would be most fitting in naming the congregation's experience of transgenerational suffering and shame as well as God's covenant promise of deliverance from it.

- How the presence of God's new covenant in human hearts will incline us to obedience and "cure our bent to sinning," as Charles Wesley composed.[3] What will be stopped? What will start? What does obedience require?

- Obedience demonstrates that we know our God and our God knows us. Identify specific actions and effects of God's new covenant rooting in your context.

- God is full of hope for what, how, and with whom we will plant and build. What partnerships are already in place? What potential partnerships are on the horizon? What future awaits to be built with God? Boldly cast a vision of God's preferred future in your context.

Ideas for Preaching on Luke 18:1-8

The Reverend Dr. Martin Luther King, Jr. preached in the National Cathedral in Washington D.C.: "The arc of the moral universe is long but bends towards justice."[4] Where the arc touches the ground is well beyond the horizon; it is well beyond the portion of the horizon that God has placed and asked us to serve and tend for this season. And yet it is there, reaching, persisting, and magnetizing the faithful towards it. There will inevitably be bumps and delays. There will be forces intent to undermine so that we forgo. There may be a justice we give our life's vocation for, or even our very lives for just like king, and still not see the consummation. Even so, those offerings are holy, needful, and transformative. Those offerings matter as they ensure a more just future by working towards justice while inspiring others in the present. King was right; God has already determined that the universe will be more just and equitable in the end. The choice is ours as to what help or hindrance we contribute in God's plan.

Conversations about justice are incomplete without reflections upon power and privilege. In this parable, the judge is the majority and has worldly power and privilege. He is established in profession and the community. He is connected to influencers. His word interprets governance that impacts the governed. He has means. He is educated. He is accustomed to the respect afforded his voice and his office. Conversely, when a woman was identified as a widow in scripture, it was not just a designation that her spouse had died. This designation resonated with destitution. Widows were without help or kin. They had no one to advocate for them. They were often left to beg. Many were unhoused. Together, these circumstances isolated widows; and when segments within a population become isolated, they also become targets.

Bringing the Text to Life

In moving from text to sermon, consider what Jesus's parable teaches about the nature of justice and justice work. Reflect on the justice work, the opportunities for justice work, and the character traits to be curated to pursue justice work in your context.

The widow Jesus casts in this parable is without privilege; however, she is not without power. She uses her faith and her voice ceaselessly. Each time she addresses the judge, she communicates to one and all her value, agency, and dignity. She would not give up on what was right or give up on herself. By the world's standards, she is deficient. By kingdom standards, she is an example of relentless persistence and quiet confidence in the face of empire. Through her, Jesus teaches that justice can be ours, that we must commit to that truth and work towards it, no matter what.

The widow's resolve of perseverance overtime grates against current appetites for instant gratification. We hear *the things that are worth it are worth working for*, and yet we can grow weary in the working. We wonder when enough is enough. Is this a lost cause? Are we running without purpose or beating air as the Apostle Paul feared (1 Corinthians 9:26)? Justice seekers consistently answer resistance with resilience. They persevere in prayer. They do not lose heart. They believe that God is capable of justice and already at work towards it. They join God in this work so that when the Son of Man returns, he will not have to wonder if he will find such faith. He will know.

Notes

October 26, 2025–Twentieth Sunday after Pentecost

Joel 2:23-32; Psalm 65; 2 Timothy 4:6-8, 16-18; *Luke 18:9-14*

Sarah B. Miller

Preacher to Preacher Prayer

Speak, Lord, your servant is listening. Speak what is true. Amen.

Ideas for Preaching on Joel 2:23-32

The closing words of Joel 2 are full of God's compassion and promise. After a lengthy description of the fearsome Day of the Lord and a call to repentance, the prophet foretells a vision of God's empathy permeating and transforming all of creation. Everything from personal harvest to communal honor will experience restoration and renewal (vv. 23-24, 26). It will be a time of protection and prosperity. The prophet's instruction is clear: pay attention and be ready for "the LORD is about to do great things" (2:21)!

Bringing the Text to Life

In moving from text to sermon this week, consider God's vision foretold by Joel, and then begin articulating God's vision for your congregation. Reflect upon what it would look like in your context for God's compassion and promise to be in completion. What questions would be answered? What needs fulfilled? What justices established? What partnerships launched?

Identify the raw materials and valuable assets already in your midst. It is to our detriment to only name what we *need* without praising what and who God has *already* provided. We are a people of expectant hope. We are a people who live our most faithful lives in the in-between of "already and not yet." We believe God is already at work doing great things, and we believe that God has great things yet to come. It is a wonder and a miracle to be in relationship with this transformational God. We are in relation because of God's invitation. *That* great thing is the wellspring of every other potential great thing.

Additionally, consider inviting the congregation to explore their own story, noticing their personal experience of and participation in making God's vision real and timely. How is what they are dreaming and envisioning part of God's plan (v. 28)? This is an invitation to reflect on one's vocation. Fredrick Buechner profoundly defined vocation in these words: "The place God calls you to is the place where your deep gladness and the world's deep hunger meet."[5]

We followers of God are at our best when there is genuine continuity between our vocation and our identity, between who we say we are and what we do. We are at our best when we incarnate God's vision as and into vocation, individually as well as communally. And we are able, because God is faithful in pouring out God's transformative spirit again and again.

When we live with genuine continuity between our vocation and identity, there will be no doubt that God is in our midst (v. 27). There will be no doubt that all creation belongs to God. And there will be no doubt that God's individual invitations to do good things have led us communally and vocationally in being part of God's great things, those underway and those yet to come.

Ideas for Preaching on Luke 18:9-14

This passage is additional evidence of the "great reversal" announced by Jesus's incarnation. The "wonderful, joyous news for all people" born in Bethlehem intentionally initiates the last being first, the lowly exalted, the guilty forgiven, and the lost found and connected by Jesus to a community of believers (Luke 2:10).

The good news of Jesus's great reversal stirred up controversy because it "draws the circle wider." There are no outsiders to Jesus's mission, ministry, or love, as evidenced in his gospel teachings and interactions.

The good news of Jesus's great reversal that draws the circle wider has kingdom impact—not just because of what Jesus did, but also because of how we, the Church, are to redirect and repurpose our mission, ministry, and love in response to what Jesus did so that we also include who Jesus included. This is the faithful foundation and expectation we inherit from Jesus. And yet, how quickly the faithful can stumble in following humbly.

The difference in the prayers of the Pharisee and the tax collector reveals the differing contents of their hearts as well as their differing attitudes towards God and neighbor. As a student and teacher of the Law, as a leader in the community, one would think the Pharisee would "talk the talk" and "walk the walk" of loving God and loving neighbor. His arrogant, prideful, and slanderous prayer evidences the contrary.

In this parable, Jesus positions specific words, hearts, and attitudes in two distinct characters. It is important for readers and preachers alike to hold space for our words, hearts, and attitudes being like that of either the tax collector or the Pharisee. The hope of Jesus's great reversal in us and through us is that our wills would be bent and our hearts would be shaped like that of the repentant tax collector.

The tax collector asks God for mercy, naming himself a sinner. In asking to be set apart from his sin through forgiveness, the tax collector boldly asks God to be set apart as a visible demonstration of the transformative power of the Holy Spirit in the community. The Holy Spirit's transformative power in love leads us in lifting up rather than looking down on our neighbors. Recall these words from 1 John 4:20-21, "Those who say, 'I love God' and hate their brothers or sisters are liars. After all, those who don't love their brothers or sisters whom they have seen can hardly love God whom they have not seen! This commandment we have from him: Those who claim to love God ought to love their brother and sister also."

Bringing the Text to Life

In moving from text to sermon this week, it serves us well to reflect on these questions:

- How can we love God if we are so full of ourselves?

- How can we love our neighbors if we see only their sinful shortcomings?

- What good is meticulous obedience to commandments if it does not lead the church in nurturing relationships in the present and coming kingdom?

- What is the relationship between humility and repentance, and what long-term positive effect can they have on Christ followers' lives as well as the future of the church?

Notes

November 2, 2025–All Saints Sunday

Daniel 7:1-3, 15-18; *Psalm 149; Ephesians 1:11-23; **Luke 6:20-31***

Sarah B. Miller

Preacher to Preacher Prayer

Speak, Lord, your servant is listening. Speak what is true. Amen.

Ideas for Preaching on Daniel 7:1-3, 15-18

As I was growing up in Florida, tropical storms were common in early June. One year a tropical storm was right off the coast the first day of vacation Bible school. The wind and rain howled outside as children enjoyed their morning rotating through study and fellowship experiences. The executive pastor at the church determined we would close and cancel Tuesday of VBS, which was a bluebird Florida day. The joke became, "Better cancel tomorrow; it's raining somewhere off the coast." It is always raining somewhere off the coast. There is always some horrible thing going on somewhere, and how we react to that truth demonstrates our trust and confidence in the Lord.

The book of Daniel chronicles one calamity after the other, and in each, the underdog wins. Shadrach, Meshach, and Abednego survive the fiery furnace (chap. 3). Daniel emerges from the lion's den unscathed (chap. 6). Political, religious, and societal forces swirl in clouds of crisis and drama, seeking to suck in the prophet and tear him down. Daniel is steadfast because the Lord is steadfast.

From Daniel 7 forward, the prophetic text takes on a much more apocalyptic nature, complete with robust and dynamic eschatological visions. Even so, the prophet provides consistent messaging: there will likely be one calamity after another, and in each, the underdog wins. Be it the short game or the long game, with the One True God, the underdog always wins.

Bringing the Text to Life

In moving from text to sermon this week, consider for your context, "what troubles have we seen, what conflicts have we passed, what fighting without, and fears within, since we assembled last?"[1] In identifying those troubles, what words of comfort ought to be shared? What truth-telling ought to take place? What response-in-progress can be identified and articulated? What unknown resources have become known, and celebrated?

It is essential for sermons that examine hardships to resist minimizing and/or deflecting pain. It is also essential that these sermons drive towards and conclude with hope that is both encouraging and strategic. There will be people hearing this message who are ready to act, while others will be ready to reflect. Some will be brave in facing the hardship head on, while others will be brave in saying "Not today." All of this is holy work that our God receives as an offering and is a testament to God's set-apart people taking active roles in shaping the moral arc of history.

It is true that we will surely find what we seek: negative for negative and positive for positive. Seeking and naming the good in the midst of the calamity interrupts established patterns of only seeing the negative. That interruption is a gift, recalling us to the hope and good already present within and around us. The knowledge that God's people have experienced hardship before and God saw them through fortifies us. We may very well be confused by the apocalypticism in Daniel, and we can be confident that God is with us, just like Daniel. It is true that "weeping may stay all night, but by morning, joy" (Psalm 30:5). Learning from those who have gone before us helps dry our tears, encourage our hearts, and empower our wills in the present towards a more hopeful future.

Ideas for Preaching on Luke 6:20-31

What is the good life and how do we get there? Is it a life of personal pleasure? Is it a life spent in service to others? Is it a life free from work and complicated relationships? Is it a life of working to make complicated relationships whole?

A glaring problem with "the good life" is that society tempts us with is its transitory and fleeting nature, which is why some folk find themselves always on the run after the next thing and the next and the next. While new and exciting things can and do shift our present emotional states—often towards the positive—what is left when the newness fades?

Jesus is the invitation to the good life that God offers, and when we are in relationship with Jesus, the newness never fades. Persons maturing as Christ followers enjoy a greater sense of meaning and purpose in their lives. These folks are affected when new and exciting things can and do shift their present emotional states; and when the newness fades, they remain at peace. These folks experience struggle and strain, and they understand that enduring and overcoming through Christ-like actions are key ways to make meaning in this life and contribute to society.

The sermon on the plain is Jesus's greatest consecutive teaching on the ethic of care and the "upside-down" nature of God's present and coming kingdom in the Third Gospel. Jesus's message is clear: we do not have to live the way we are currently living or function the way society currently functions. There is another way to be. It will appear as foolishness to some, as the Apostle Paul would later write; however, living this way incarnates faithfulness to the highest degree (1 Corinthians 1:18).

Bringing the Text to Life

In moving from text to sermon this week, consider:

- Images of restoration in this text and their relationship to resilience. Restoration does not come with being removed from the tensions and hardships in life, but rather by demonstrating there is another, more Christ-like way to live in the midst of and in response to them.

- Acts, images, and leaders of nonviolent restorative justice, such as civil rights and anti-apartheid movement leaders, abolitionists, and those committed to the ongoing reconciliation work following the troubles in Northern Ireland. Seek examples on the local level, too, in your own community and church. Stories are phenomenal teachers, and when stories lift up lessons in our own neighborhood, our awareness and our hearts shift.

- What does it look like to love your enemies? It looks like being a generous and curious listener. It looks like trying on new perspectives and hanging in the tension rather than running from it. It looks like creating space and pausing in grace when an ideal or practice is not for you; a difference of opinion or belief does not have to equate to stigmatization, fear, or loss of relationship. Search out other scriptural examples that further illumine and contextualize Jesus's instruction, such as in 1 John 3:11-18.

- Frances Bacon, English philosopher and Lord High Chancellor, wrote, "It is not what men eat, but what they digest that makes them strong; not what we gain, but what we save that makes us rich; not what we read, but what we remember that makes us learned; not what we preach or pray, but what we practice and believe that makes us Christians."[2] Jesus shows us the beautifully messy way to the good life, the holy life. It is up to us if, when, and how we follow.

Notes

November 9, 2025–
Twenty-Second Sunday after
Pentecost

Haggai 1:15b-2:9; *Psalm 145:1-5, 17-21*; *Job 19:23-27a*; *Psalm 17:1-9*;
2 Thessalonians 2:1-5, 13-17; *Luke 20:27-38*

Sarah B. Miller

Preacher to Preacher Prayer

Speak, Lord, your servant is listening. Speak what is true. Amen.

Ideas for Preaching on Haggai 1:15b-2:9

The exiled children of Israel have come home. Reconstruction efforts on the Temple started, but now enthusiasm has waned. God calls forth the prophet Haggai to address the people about their priorities.

Haggai's first question is one of nostalgia: "Remember the good ole days . . . Remember Camelot . . .?" When we think in terms of nostalgic memories, we think of our best days—be it as individuals or as a congregation—as being behind us rather than ahead. This thinking shortchanges us and also shortchanges our belief in what God has in store for us. It is important to answer nostalgia questions, to give thanks for where we have been and who helped us on our way. It is also essential that individuals as well as organizations progress into the future and not just pine for the past. If we resist adaptation and innovation, we die.

Haggai's second question is loaded and thrusts hearers back to reality. Rose-colored glasses off, filters eliminated, sentimentality removed. How does the Temple look to you now? How does the Temple look to you really? Here, *Temple* bears a double implication: the first being the physical structure and the second being the quality of God's people's experience of community. Both are unfinished. Stalled. On the backburner. Not a priority. And the supporting evidence to that effect glares. Individuals and organizations struggle. Individuals and organizations face adversaries. Even so, the spirit of God is in us and with us. Therefore, we can take courage. Therefore, we can not fear. Therefore, we can get to work.

Haggai's final question is a challenge to and/or critique of the community's work. Of the prophet's three questions, this is the only "yes/no" question. It is a question of awareness and accountability. The community's deficient and stalled work on the Temple's reconstruction speaks loudly to the community's deficient and stalled work on reuniting in focus and faith as God's people. Back on home turf, the demands of life became distractions, resulting in tunnel vision rather than Temple vision. Without vision, God's people lost sight of the Temple's purpose—the gathering place of God's children for prayer, praise, and preparation for the care of neighbor and creation.

Bringing the Text to Life

In moving from text to sermon this week, consider and then craft responses based on your context to the three questions the prophet asks God's people in verse 3. This passage concludes with a hopeful image of the eschatological Temple. This new creation will result cooperatively. God will do this, and we are invited to be part of it. This invitation necessitates realigning our paths, purposes, and priorities with God's. This invitation necessitates taking initiative, holding one another accountable, and cultivating community. We as God's people are at our best when we are united in focus and faith, when we are shaped by our past, transformed in this present, and serve as one towards God's preferred future.

Ideas for Preaching on 2 Thessalonians 2:1-5, 13-17

There are nineteen questions—known as Wesley's historic questions—that every Methodist pastor has been asked since 1773 prior to their admission into an Annual Conference. The *action* in all nineteen questions is a form of the verb "to be": *Will you . . . / Are you . . . Do you . . . / Have you . . . .* Questions predicated on a form of the verb "to be" are always and only answered with a "yes" or a "no."

There is something to be said about Wesley's historic questions taking a yes/no response form. And it is this: "Let your *yes* mean yes, and your *no* mean no" (Matthew 5:37). Wesley's questions call for honesty. They heave with accountability. Because if pastors are intended to lead faith communities in the steps of becoming real Christ followers—those who worship God in Spirit and in truth—then it better begin with them. It better begin with us.

One of Wesley's nineteen questions resonates deeply with a concept from this Scripture passage: do you expect to be made perfect in love in this life? This question is a balm in Gilead, a salve for a sin-sick soul. This question tells us the end of the story; because of sin, humanity fell; but friends, because of Christ, we will rise in glory.

Wesley detailed his understanding of grace in his teachings on the *Via Salutis* or *Way of Salvation*. Humanity was created in God's image; we were created good and perfect. We abused God's good gift of free will and therefore fell from perfection, but, friends, we did not fall from grace. Some Christian traditions teach that when humanity fell, we landed in a pit of total depravity. Drawing upon the (practically) immortal words of Lee Corso, "not so fast!" Not so fast, neighboring Christian traditions, not so fast! The Wesleyan tradition believes we are not in a pit of total depravity because of God's grace. God's grace is with us always, elevating us, lifting us, going before us, preparing us to choose to pursue God with our lives. Once we make that choice, God's grace nourishes and sustains our choice.

The "working together" with God over our lifetime in the security of grace-filled wings is the work of sanctification. God's sanctifying grace that heartens, hems in, and holds accountable, altogether helps us once again realize and bring to life the image in which we were created. The work of sanctification makes us holy, and being made holy is only possible by drawing close to that which is holy by first, being encountered by the holy; second, observing the thoughts and actions of the holy; and third, incorporating the behavior of the holy in one's own life.

Bringing the Text to Life

In moving from text to sermon this week, reflect upon your personal journey with God's grace or upon another's journey with God's grace. What do you notice in that experience of Christian formation? In God's grace acting upon the soul and the soul reacting upon God's grace? In what specific ways did God go ahead of them, make them right and new, and curate holiness within them and from them "in every good thing [they] do or say" (v. 17)? If you share your own story, ensure you are not the hero of your story. If you share another's story, take care to have their permission or to share in a way that puts them at ease. The work of sanctification is by no means a perfect process, but we believe through sanctification we will be perfect in the end.

Notes

November 16, 2025– Twenty-Third Sunday after Pentecost

Isaiah 65:17-25; *Psalm 98; 2 Thessalonians 3:6-13; **Luke 21:5-19***

Andy Whitaker-Smith

Preacher to Preacher Prayer

Dear Lord, thank you for the gift of scripture and the comfort and strength these two familiar texts provide. May we continue to experience ways they call us to live life and follow you today. Help us to open ourselves to your richness, and share with each other.

Ideas for Preaching on Isaiah 65:17-25

We may sometimes feel like we have to "spice up" the Hebrew Bible/Old Testament, unless it's a passage about war and violence. These kinds of bite-sized perceptions about the Old Testament—emphasis on the *Old*—can continue an assumption in churches that the Hebrew Bible isn't as engaging as the Gospels. But if we remember the rich poetry these ancient writings offer, and especially a God responding to the needs of the people time and time again, how might that help us think of the needs we and our congregations have today? Who is in need of a God to answer them and with news of hope? Who needs to hear that new things are being created as a joy, that there will be no more sounds of weeping? Are we listening?

In the film *Superman Returns*, Superman comes back to earth after five years. Most are glad to see him, but one who's not is reporter and love interest Lois Lane, who has won an award for an editorial titled "Why the World Doesn't Need Superman." When he asks her why she wrote it, she says, "Because the world doesn't need a savior." So, Superman flies her up over the city of Metropolis and asks her what she hears, and she says she can't hear anything. Superman says: "I hear everything. You wrote that the world doesn't need a savior. But every day I hear people crying for one." Who in your congregation and community needs to know their cries have been heard?

This text of Isaiah is a wonderful example to counter the assumption that the God of the Old Testament is always angry and vengeful. Here we are reminded of what can happen after a long period of uncertainty and even suffering—darkness gives way to light, and crying gives way to rejoicing. It may feel like a chore, sometimes, to try and paint this in a new way to a congregation that may feel comfortable enough in their surroundings. But preach this passage in a homeless shelter, or a recovery group, or around a circle of widows and widowers. Are we preaching good news to the ones who truly need to hear it?

And what about you, Preacher? How have *you* experienced new creation or healing through God? Do your people know that story?

Bringing the Text to Life

* What examples of new creation could you celebrate around your church? New people? New groups? New ministries?

* What new things are happening in your community? How might your church partner with them?

* How have people experienced healing in your community? How might you offer healing or response to those in need?

* Show this clip from *Superman Returns*, and ask how your church could make listening a spiritual practice.

* Invite some of your members to share stories of how they've experienced new creation in their lives from God, or how God responded to them in a time of need.

Ideas for Preaching on Luke 21:5-19

This is one of those passages when Jesus really seems like a party pooper. I can just imagine the disciples and maybe some other folk walking out of the temple, saying things such as, "Such a nice service. Such a nice day. Oh, what beautiful stonework. Don't we have such a lovely temple?" And then Jesus coming up behind them and just killing the mood. Can we just have one moment when you don't ruin things by speaking so divinely?

But we often prefer to focus on the "pleasant" things. And it's not even that Jesus never did that; in fact, he may have done so more than anyone, speaking of the enjoyment of lilies, birds, sheep, bread, seeds, children—simple realities of this world that we can and should enjoy, because that's part of the kingdom of God. Perhaps the difference is Jesus is not satisfied with only speaking of these pleasant and cheerful realities, but knows that we must also speak into the reality of what it costs for us to be the kingdom of God.

The idea and even the word *persecution* continues to grow in our American culture. People feel they must defend their beliefs, values, or way of life because other forces are trying to take them away or replace them. At the time of this writing, several states have enacted legislation to guard some of those beliefs and values, so that all residents must live by them. Perhaps a way to test if we're truly being persecuted is to ask ourselves: *Am I still allowed to be who I am, or do I not like that others are trying to be who they want to be?* Being told that we don't have a say in how individuals or communities choose to live or identify themselves may feel as though our values or beliefs are being persecuted, but there's a difference between grumbling about how things are changing and not feeling safe to go out into one's own community.

This was the divide Jesus was often in, and he spoke of how standing up for those who needed sanctuary would often be costly. Are we willing to preach truths and realities that may result in comments other than "Good sermon"? When was the last time it truly cost us something to follow Jesus—other than long committee meetings or dealing with drama in our congregations?

Since we are in an age where we are reporting more statistics and metrics of church attendance and engagement, it may be eye-opening to realize that these weren't great during Jesus's time either. Some days it was thousands of people, but usually it was only because they were expecting him to say something profound or do something miraculous; but when he started speaking truths such as "I am the Bread" and "Love your enemies," people didn't want to hear it. We can offer a lot of advice for "successful preaching" like hooks and rhythms and presence; but we all know there will be those sermons that come down to *what are you willing to give up to follow Jesus?*

Bringing the Text to Life

- What are some "nice things" in your church that Jesus's prediction of coming down one day might catch your congregation's attention?

- What's your church's track record of attendance and engagement in the last year? How does it compare with the track record of Jesus's followers and participants in Gospel stories?

- What needs do you see in your community that, if you spoke of them in the pulpit, might result in disapproval, or even persecution from the congregation? What times in your church's history has your congregation or former pastors gone in a direction that was opposed by others? How might those stories help speak to what is needed in our current season?

Notes

November 23, 2025–
Twenty-Fourth Sunday after
Pentecost

Jeremiah 23:1-6; *Psalm 46; Colossians 1:11-20;* **Luke 23:33-43**

Andy Whitaker-Smith

Preacher to Preacher Prayer

Gracious God, Lord, and King, may we know the true kingdom you present, on earth as it is in heaven; and may we live that kingdom with you and with each other.

Ideas for Preaching on Jeremiah 23:1-6

Though it may seem an odd time in our secular calendar, Reign of Christ—or Christ the King—Sunday marks the end of our liturgical calendar. On the cusp of Thanksgiving and in the middle of our holiday seasons, we find ourselves remembering what our liturgical and religious calendars have been preparing us for all year: Christ is the King. And what kind of king is Christ?

As followers of Christ, we look at the Hebrew Bible (aka Old Testament) with certain lenses, connecting the predictions and prophecies mentioned with Jesus, as we will begin celebrating, soon, in the days of Advent. The king we have been waiting for will finally arrive, and we are given glimpses of how that king will reign. What does it mean that the book of Jeremiah describes this king with images of shepherds and branches? The references to the current shepherds misleading and abusing their flocks paint the picture of the oppression the Israelites are facing, and that the true king will rule in a different way. Does this speak to some who may currently be in power? What are we doing in our communities to speak to those who are being mistreated and oppressed? Which shepherds are we?

This passage in Jeremiah could be connected not just with the selected text of Luke 23, but Matthew 25 as well, in the image of sheep—where they are led and how they are treated. Are we leading others to paths of sanctuary, where they will be loved and welcomed; or are we showing a leadership of judgement and condemnation, that this is how Christ rules?

Jeremiah describes this righteous branch as the means of executing justice. Connecting to the Reign of Christ—if that reign, that kingdom, is here and near to us, the incarnation of Christ, physically on this earth—is a command that we are to live justice amongst each other. The ways we do this can be many; how might this work in your congregation? What opportunities can your church take?

As we approach the Thanksgiving holiday, how might we usher in the Reign of Christ, this year, with an attitude of thanks? How do we thank a king who rules with wisdom, grace, and justice? What are ways we imitate these gifts?

Bringing the Text to Life

- The film *Ben-Hur* (1959) shows one of the most powerful portrayals of Jesus in cinema—and he never says a word. Show the scene where Ben-Hur and other prisoners stop in Nazareth so the Roman soldiers can get water. The clip shows the lead soldier declaring no water for Ben-Hur, but Jesus kneels down and gives him a drink. The soldier takes out his whip to deal with them, but Jesus stands—his back to us, so that we watch the soldier's reaction. We see the soldier's strength fade and he turns away, while Ben-Hur is able to stand, strengthened. What is the difference between the power of force and the power of compassion, while also standing up for what is right?

- Include in your altar paraments and decorations visuals of branches to remind the church how they can be branches of justice and connection to each other and their community.

- If you have any Thanksgiving traditions during worship that include altar calls or coming forward, include tangible givings or commitments people could make to acts of justice in the community.

Ideas for Preaching on Luke 23:33-43

The word *anthropomorphizing* is often referred to our putting human characteristics onto animals, whether in real life or fiction. The film studio Pixar has shown how we can do the same thing not just with animals, but toys, bugs, cars, even emotions. Some have argued we can anthropomorphize God, as well. You may have seen the fairly old image, by now, of a "buff Jesus" breaking the cross he's still crucified on, snapping the horizontal pieces with his hands still nailed down. Mark Driscoll, who was then a lead pastor at megachurch Mars Hill, preached many times of his desire for Jesus to be tough because "I can't worship a god I can beat up."

As we experience this text on the Sunday that lifts up the Reign of Christ, or Christ the King Sunday, how do we anthropomorphize Jesus? What do we *place upon* him? Isn't that the whole point of Jesus being on the cross? How we see Jesus on that cross, how we see Jesus as king, determines how we worship and emulate that king. If we're looking for a king who comes in like Arnold Schwarzenegger from a 1980s movie, how do we reconcile passages such as Luke 23? How do we see a king—a savior—asking forgiveness for his enemies and telling criminals they will be with him in paradise?

Are we okay with a God we can beat up—isn't that what we did, two thousand years ago? We may say we want a "tough Jesus," a "tough God," a "tough king." At the time of this writing, there is a rise of parishioners around the U.S. telling their pastors that the words of Jesus—such as the Beatitudes—no longer work for our time because they promote weakness. Is that the kind of king we want when we're in need of forgiveness?

Imagine being on that cross, next to the "King of the Jews," for what you should not have done but did, or what you should have done but didn't. What should Jesus say on your behalf: "Toughen up" or "Father, forgive them"?

In our need of forgiveness, in a season of thanksgiving, what kind of king would we truly be thankful for: one who would break himself down from the cross or one who would stay on the cross for us?

Bringing the Text to Life

- Google the phrase "Buff Jesus" and display the photo of the character breaking the cross. Ask what reactions or feelings the congregation may have. Would some actually be relieved or empowered if Jesus was more like this?

- Show the scene from the 2006 film *Talladega Nights: The Ballad of Ricky Bobby* in which everyone is praying and starts sharing how they picture and prefer Jesus.

- Are there other illustrations of Jesus you could display as examples of how humanity puts their own desired traits upon him? Perhaps display a Warner Sallman painting that might already be in your church.

Notes

November 27, 2025–
Thanksgiving Day, USA

Deuteronomy 26:1-11; Psalm 100; Philippians 4:4-9; **John 6:25-35**

Andy Whitaker-Smith

Preacher to Preacher Prayer

Lord of all we have and receive, we give thanks to you, for the gift of life and of each other. May our thanks be embodied and lived by our following you, and sharing your abundance.

Ideas for Preaching on Deuteronomy 26:1-11

Part of the celebration of Thanksgiving is remembrance. Loved ones gather together in familiar surroundings with people they love, perhaps a full year from the last time they saw each other. Sights, sounds, and even smells can entice memories of past celebrations and continue traditions of love and sharing. This is unfortunately not everyone's experience at Thanksgiving, so it is important to be mindful of your congregation's context and the individuals listening to the message and how they come in with hopes or hesitations of this holiday. And perhaps the method of lifting up memories while acknowledging that not all of them may be positive, is showing how the people of Deuteronomy were guided to experience their own memory and heritage, and to know it was not all celebratory.

In the Israelites accessing their past oppressions, we have an opportunity to recognize those who have experienced their own challenges as part of their heritage, or perhaps some of the challenges your church has experienced over the years. Where do you find yourselves this year? Have you experienced abundance? Have you experienced gifts? Are you able to come together and give thanks for knowing God's presence among your church? Has your community experienced God's grace because of your ministries?

Another aspect of Thanksgiving for our churches can be the opportunity to reflect on how we have shown abundance, whether in a season of normalcy or, more importantly, in a season of hardship or scarcity. There's the popular experiment of handing out pizza to a crowd and saying there's a limited amount, and seeing who grabs two or three pieces so they have enough for themselves, and who only takes one so that others may have enough. In this current season, are we operating under a faith of scarcity or of abundance? What does God call us to do?

In those seasons of scarcity and certainly oppression, we can respond as God's people through actions of generosity; so that no matter how challenging or overwhelming things might be, they cannot take our commitment to each other or God. Acts of generosity show our thanks to God, who is always generous and always provides. What are ways your church can practice this kind of Thanksgiving this year?

Bringing the Text to Life

* If not already a part of your Thanksgiving tradition at your church, allow people to share stories and memories of how their congregation has gone through tough times or has been there for others during their tough times.

* Share photos on screen or around the sanctuary of the church's past. What memories might they stir? Perhaps during a time of prayer or music, the congregation can walk around and look at each of them.

* What kind of "basket of first fruits" could your congregation collect, as a part of worship? What special offering could you take up, or what new commitment of service or partnership in the community could you offer?

Ideas for Preaching on John 6:25-35

Do we truly know what we are thankful for? Do we celebrate thanks for what God has gifted the world or just "the stuff" we happen to have? Do we know the difference?

Prosperity Gospel Theology teaches that God blesses faithful followers with material possessions and tangible gifts. If we give riches towards God's service (however the speaker at the moment is describing "God's service" to be), those riches will be given back in abundance. How does this type of theology live next to a passage such as John 6, in which Jesus is surrounded by those who have received physical bread, want more, but instead hear the words of Jesus become more and more challenging by the moment? What's it like to come to Jesus when we are full versus when we are starving, and do we actually know the difference? Do we allow Jesus to explain to us the difference, or are we only listening for what we want to hear?

How do the people of the congregation hear these words? Is our church one that has experienced challenge and need, or have we been fairly comfortable and full? Whether we're hungry or satisfied as a church—as Christians—how do we find ourselves currently asking for bread, and how do we take Jesus's response that *he* is the Bread? Is our church one that needs to be reminded of what "true bread from heaven" is?

This passage of John is arguably the beginning of one of the more vulnerable scenes of Jesus in this Gospel. Helping our congregation understand the full power of what Jesus is stating of his being *the true bread of life* may be as difficult as Jesus doing so himself with the people he was surrounded by. And on Thanksgiving Day, no less, when there may be those who are checking their watches and anxious to check on their cooking, and others anxious to enjoy said cooking—how do we take the anticipation and maybe even impatience in the room and effectively communicate Jesus's own challenge: helping people see that he is the Bread?

For the way our culture and society celebrate Thanksgiving, in a reality that many in our chairs and pews already experience more abundance and sustenance than many around the rest of the planet, what is the opportunity we truly have, here, to share the good news Christ offers, to get our heads and our hearts around his declaration: "Whoever comes to me will never go hungry" (v. 35).

An additional opportunity is the beginning of the season of Advent. In a few days, churches will begin a new time of celebration and anticipation. Reminding our churches, now, that the one born on Christmas Day is the true bread and the true life can prepare us to anticipate not only the tangible gifts but also the ways we can see Christ in our lives.

Bringing the Text to Life

- If you have a tradition of a church-wide Thanksgiving meal, consider having the event before worship or at least before the message. Allow all to enjoy the meal and the physical fullness participants will feel, and then speak to the difference of that fullness to the fullness Christ truly offers. What might it be like to hear Jesus's words when our stomachs are already full?

- Communion is always a blessed ritual, but this day allows for special significance. Whether it's a formal Great Thanksgiving or a casual passing, there are few passages arguably better than John 6 to allow for a time of Communion together.

- Take the leftovers of Communion (or make sure there are extra elements) out into the community: shut-ins, assisted living facilities, homeless shelters, individuals living alone. Start a new tradition in the season of Thanksgiving of sharing the body of Christ with those in your community.

Notes

November 30, 2025–First Sunday of Advent

Isaiah 2:1-5; Psalm 122; Romans 13:11-14; **Matthew 24:36-44**

Dalton Rushing

Preacher to Preacher Prayer

Dear Lord, on this first Sunday of Advent, help me to remind the people I serve that the world-as-it-is is not yet the world-as-it-should-be. And help them to believe that, with your help, that world-as-it-should-be is possible. Amen.

Ideas for Preaching on Isaiah 2:1-5

Like the Gospel lection for today, Isaiah's vision of God's coming provides a jarring entrance into Advent for the congregation and a fun entrance into Advent for the preacher. While many people come to church on the first Sunday of Advent looking forward to the sweetness of Christmas, the preacher has an opportunity to begin with the reality of the world and the promise of God's coming.

The good news is that whether the congregation knows it or not, they need the message that Isaiah brings. Like many modern Christians, the writer of this passage may have remembered more stable times, but the circumstances of the writing were anything but stable. Much was changing. Suffering was obvious. The people needed a word from the Lord.

The beginning of verse two, "in the days to come," does a lot of work in this passage. This phrase has sometimes been translated as "in the last days," affirming the apocalyptic nature of this passage. However, it does not need to be the end of the world for this message to be true. The point, for Isaiah, is to remind his listeners of the promised hope of God's coming. This hope happens every Advent, like clockwork, just as it happens every day.

This is a Sunday for big ideas, as visions and dreams are big things. Rarely does the preacher have such an opportunity to speak so clearly and openly about the kind of world God desires. Invite the congregation into this dream. Imagine: If God had God's way, what would the world look like? How would it look similar to the world now? How would it look differently? Imagination is something of a lost art for Christians, and yet the Bible calls for it continually. If the Advent and Christmas season provide opportunities for dreaming about what could be, then this scripture demands these dreams. Ask the congregation: what would God's ideal world look like? And what is it that is keeping us from working to create that world, with God's help?

Bringing the Text to Life

A number of organizations do the work of literally beating weapons into farming tools. Find a local organization to do a demonstration, or share more about their work.

Consider Jackson Browne's "The Rebel Jesus." How does this song speak to the world of which Isaiah dreams?

Invite the congregation to write out in one hundred words or less what God's ideal world looks like, and then invite them to consider one step they could take to bridge the gap between the world as it is and the world as it should be. Perhaps include a sticky note in each person's bulletin for them to write on, and then collect the notes on the wall for people to read after the service.

Ideas for Preaching on Matthew 24:36-44

Like the Isaiah text, the Gospel passage for today presents an apocalyptic beginning to Advent. Unlike the Isaiah text, this passage does not—on the surface—present a positive view of the world as it could one day be. Instead, Jesus presents what looks like a warning: keep watch, for you do not know when God is coming. There is some good news in this warning, for Jesus tells us that the prognosticators and profiteers who make a good living reading supposed code into scripture to scare good Christian people have it entirely wrong. The day and time of God's victory is known only to God. This passage also gives a helpful backdrop to faithful Christians who struggle with the excess of the holidays in many cultures. Of course, excess will happen; this excess looks a lot like the excess that happened in Noah's day, before the story of Noah reminded God's people of what mattered in quite dramatic fashion. The point is not the excess, of course. The point is faithfulness.

This message of warning, however, goes beyond Black Friday sales and seas of wrapping paper. Preparation for the coming of God is a universally appropriate message, true across time and space. The excesses of the Advent and Christmas seasons quite ironically distract us from the most powerful message the season has to offer us: in the midst of all that tries to distract us, God has come to be with us, living among us, as one of us. Being alert is not about protecting your own hide. Being alert is about looking for signs of the holy in the midst of a season that has corrupted the concept of what is holy. What is more, being prepared to enter God's presence can only be truly accomplished if we are willing to do the work of believing that the message of Christmas is actually true: God with us. Emmanuel.

This passage has been used to scare so many people throughout the history of the church. Consider the ways in which the main subject of the speech from Jesus might not be the one who didn't pay attention, but rather the one who did. What might be gained by paying attention? What might it cost?

Bringing the Text to Life

Invite the congregation to consider a time in which they had to prepare for something: a storm, a baby, a new job. What emotions did they feel? How did they address the change?

Tell the stories of those who had to keep watch: a ship captain, a shepherd, a police officer. How might their very practical strategies for paying attention teach the rest of us to look for signs of God at work?

Ask the congregation to consider its relationship with time. How does it think about time? How valuable is time for the people to whom you are preaching? How might time inform our own priorities, including the ways we live out our faith in Christ?

Notes

December 7, 2025–Second Sunday of Advent

Isaiah 11:1-10: Psalm 72:1-7, 18-19: **Romans 15:4-13; Matthew 3:1-12**

Dalton Rushing

Preacher to Preacher Prayer

God of all people, just as a voice emerges from the wilderness, I am preparing to use my voice to share your love. Bless this mess, such that those who hear this word will experience a fresh inbreaking of your spirit. Amen.

Ideas for Preaching on Romans 15:4-13

Advent can feel like a slog that is for church-going Christians alone, but the good news is that this dynamic is not new. The feelings Christians get in Advent are the same feelings that Paul's readers in the first century got: feelings of frustration and impatience; feelings of needing to care for their own during a difficult time. These feelings are legitimate now, and they certainly were legitimate then, as Paul's readers waited for the coming of the Messiah.

Really, the connections between the early church and the modern church are uncanny. The Roman church was divided between the "strong" and the "weak," echoing modern theological disagreements. There were burning questions about who counted as "in" and who counted as "out," as in modern time. And there was frustration that the problems of the church were not being resolved; one wonders what Paul would say to a church still frustrated, all these two thousand years later.

Of course, it is the preacher's job to imagine what Paul would say. And in doing so, the preacher has an opportunity to frame modern discontent, division, and desire as theological issues, not merely practical ones, as they make an appearance each Advent. How might Paul's message resonate this year? For starters, it seems likely that Paul's take on the "war on Christmas" would be that the division between those who say "Merry Christmas" and those who say "Happy Holidays" (or nothing at all!) is much less important than pundits would have us think. The point of Advent and Christmas is not some self-protective season in which only Christians indulge in celebration. The point is the coming of Christ: the great uniter.

And though Advent is merely four weeks long, there is another opportunity for the preacher to share a message about holy patience. In an instant-gratification culture, that which helps us endure four weeks can also help us endure longer periods of waiting: waiting in a hospital bed for healing, waiting for grief to become less blinding, waiting for a difficult season to pass. Paul's message to the Roman church is just as meaningful today. Yes, there is waiting. But waiting gives time to prepare. We prepare because we believe God is at work, now, even as we wait for God's coming. This is the source of our hope.

Bringing the Text to Life

- Consider making very specific connections between the modern contexts of contemporary life and the ancient concepts Paul shares in this passage. How might these principles help the congregation navigate Advent and beyond?

- Share stories in which divisions that initially seemed inevitable ended up falling away in the face of connecting points. Remind the congregation that Christ is the great connector

- There is a theme of welcome in this passage that is due exploration. How might we welcome others into the life of faith, in the same way that Mary welcomed Christ?

Ideas for Preaching on Matthew 3:1-12

Every Advent, cousin John shows up in ways that feel predictable and inconvenient at the same time. His arrival is predictable, in that he arrives each year on the second Sunday of Advent, though he is brought to dinner by Matthew, Luke, or Mark depending on the year. One simply cannot not engage in a lectionary-driven Advent without meeting John on week two. And yet even though John the Baptist shows up each Advent, his arrival feels inconvenient. For one, we already introduced the whole concept of Jesus's coming on Advent 1. It can be a challenge for preachers to reintroduce something two weeks in a row without feeling like we are simply rehashing last week's sermon. What's more, in a season in which the church is waiting for the birth of Christ, it is jarring to meet full-grown John, whose story is told after the story of Jesus's birth in both Matthew and Luke. But the real inconvenience comes from John's message. There is a reason most nativity sets and Christmas cards do not include a figure of John the Baptist! Some years ago, a cheeky friend sent me an Advent card with a dark, angry figure on the front, featuring a quote from verse seven: "You children of snakes! Who warned you to escape from the angry judgment that is coming soon?" (v. 7). The inside of the card invited me to have a "brooding and penitent" Advent.

In fact, it is the manner in which John tells us to prepare which makes his arrival difficult. Quoting Isaiah, John reminds the church that the way we prepare for the coming of God is by making God's paths straight. And if there were to be any question about what he meant, John's dramatic speech in the verses following makes it clear. Produce fruit worthy of repentance. Get your house in order. Jesus is serious about this! The hard news is that John is talking about real work. Repentance is hard work, and it is work that touches all areas of our lives, inside and out. The good news is that Jesus's burning and threshing are not being done out of retribution, but out of a desire to help in the work of repentance. After all, repentance is about straightening God's paths, about cleansing ourselves in preparation for the coming of the Lord. The burning of the husks and the clearing of the forest that Jesus will do allow for a more productive forest and a sack of wheat less likely to be spoiled. Sometimes, the hard news is the best news. Sometimes, the least convenient guest provides the strongest message of hope.

Bringing the Text to Life

- John the Baptist is an evocative figure. Help the congregation imagine what he looked like, sounded like, and smelled like.

- Think of Advent 2 as a dinner party. When was a time in which a person you were dreading actually ended up speaking life to you?

- Consider this theme of inconvenience. How might God's timing help us frame our own timing?

Notes

December 14, 2025–Third Sunday of Advent

Isaiah 35:1-10; Psalm 146:5-10; *Luke 1:46b-55*; James 5:7-10:
Matthew 11:2-11

Dalton Rushing

Preacher to Preacher Prayer

O God, speak into this dry land. Water my soul so that I may speak the truth of Advent. Remind me of the great power that you provide, and help those who hear this word remember that there is no situation so remote that you cannot find us. Thanks be to God. Amen.

Ideas for Preaching on Isaiah 35:1-10

It is interesting that on the Sunday that includes Mary's Song, the Magnificat, as a Gospel reading, the Common English Bible's section heading for the Isaiah lection is "Fertile Wilderness." How can a wilderness be fertile? Of course, there's only one way: with God's help. In many ways, this is the promise of Advent: in a world that can often feel dry and sparse, God promises more. Beyond "magnificent desolation" (as Buzz Aldrin described the moon upon landing on it in Apollo 11), God's world involves water pooling from the driest places, fountains and streams, lush pasture and productive farmland.

If this were the only message of Isaiah 35, it would be well-received, and it would be enough. And yet there is more to this passage. The extravagance that accompanies God's redemption of creation does not exist simply for the sake of existing. This extravagance is the backdrop for the unveiling of a new road, called "the Holy Way." This road is clear ("even fools won't get lost on it"), it is safe ("no predator will go up on it"), and it is meant for God's people's return to the source of all creation ("the LORD's ransomed ones will return and enter Zion with singing, with everlasting joy upon their heads") (vv. 8-10).

Is there anything we need more than a road that leads directly to God, especially in the Advent season? In a culture that so often misses the true meaning of Christmas, in a time where so many institutions seem to be falling apart, I struggle to imagine anything that could be better news than what the prophet describes in Isaiah 35. Not only will the dry world be made fertile, but God has promised a direct route for the faithful to access God. Isaiah called this "the Holy Way." In just a few days, the church will discover that another name for "the Holy Way" is "Jesus."

Bringing the Text to Life

- This text offers a myriad of opportunities to talk about nature as a metaphor for the Christian life. Consider having a conversation with a naturalist or a farmer. How do they understand seasons in their work? How do they understand hope?

- Without falling into the trap of bringing Christmas to fruition prematurely, consider the ways in which the coming of Christ allows for a direct line between earth and heaven.

- Consider the imagery of the highway. What are the roads on which we drive, and where do they lead?

Ideas for Preaching on Luke 1:46b-55

One of the consistent themes throughout the Gospel message is surprise. Even as God tells Mary who Jesus will be, even as Jesus tells his listeners what will happen to him, surprising elements fill the Gospel. There's a reason that in Clarence Jordan's retelling of the Gospels as if they had happened in the American South during the twentieth century, the character of Jesus rises from the grave and shares his first words: "Ta-da!"

Of course, the fact of Jesus's impending birth was a surprise to Mary, but after two thousand Christmases, it is not so much a surprise to the church anymore. But what may be a surprise—or at least, what feels like a surprise—is the content in Mary's song celebrating the coming Christ child. Known as the "Magnificat," this song—a psalm, really—does several things. First, Mary shares her delight at being used by God in this way. Second, she praises God for God's mercy and strength, even in the midst of her life as a subject in an oppressive regime. Third, she celebrates the ways in which God will transform the world. And fourth, she gives thanks that God's promises are trustworthy.

Any of the four themes of this song are well worth preaching. Each carries within it its own bit of good news and its own surprise. But perhaps the most surprising element of this song, at least to contemporary ears, is the force with which Mary celebrates the coming transformation of the world. In a season that at its best is prone to sentimentality and at its worst is prone to kitsch, Mary enters the chat with a powerful ode to God's promise to "[pull] the powerful down from their thrones and [lift] up the lowly" (v. 52). This promise is no theoretical one, couched in metaphor. It is a promise to change the whole order of things, to scatter the arrogant, to fill the bellies of the hungry, and to cast out the rich. It is striking to hear this promise in the midst of the month of the year that sees the most economic activity! In God's world—and indeed, in Mary's—the measure of a good Christmas is not the number of presents under the tree or the amount of money spent at stores. The measure of a good Christmas is, in fact, quite the opposite: one that honors the God who raises the lowly and casts aside the rich. This is, of course, good news; it isn't gospel if it isn't good news. But it will inevitably sound like bad news to those who have bought into the great lie that people are best served by showering them with physical gifts rather than spiritual ones.

There is a danger here. Hearers of this difficult though life-giving message may try to buy their way out of it by adding a little bit to their tithe or purchasing a few presents for a child in need or giving a little more money to charity. These are good things! But they are as saccharine is to sugar: something one does to experience a similar-enough feeling to the real thing, while bypassing the real thing entirely. The hard news is that Mary's song points to the deficiencies in our practices. The good news is that Mary reminds us of God's promise to transform the world in love.

Bringing the Text to Life

- Consider using Jackson Browne's song, "The Rebel Jesus," as part of worship.

- Speak about the ways in which we "miss the forest for the Christmas trees." Invite the congregation to consider the ways in which their favorite Advent and Christmas practices bear witness to their faith. This is a Sunday for hard questions! If Jesus came to Christmas dinner, what would he think?

Notes

December 21, 2025–Fourth Sunday of Advent

Isaiah 7:10-16; **Psalm 80:1-7, 17-19**; Romans 1:1-7; **Matthew 1:18-25**

Dalton Rushing

Preacher to Preacher Prayer

Faithful God, I step out again this week into a broken world to share a word from you. Remind me this week of Joseph's bravery and steadfastness in the face of difficult circumstances. Give me courage to do the same. Give us all courage to do the same. Amen.

Ideas for Preaching on Psalm 80:1-7, 17-19

This is a psalm of longing, and as such, it sits perfectly on the fourth Sunday of Advent. We've been preparing for weeks. Christmas is days away, and we can almost smell the roast and the baked goods. But first, we arrive for worship.

Of course, the longing of the psalmist isn't the same longing we feel for Christmas, or is it? It may not be a desire for the holiday to hurry up and get here, but it is an earnest appeal for the coming of God. "Restore us, God! Make your face shine so that we can be saved!" the psalmist writes in verse three. The writer then goes into pretty harsh allegations against the God of all creation. This is someone who has experienced great pain and loss. The psalmist is, indeed, human.

Despite the heartache that the psalmist has experienced, however, the writer never turns against God, not even in anger. God is always the solution, even if the psalmist feels God's absence. God is always the source of restoration. The psalmist always desires God's face to shine.

The fourth Sunday of Advent arrives just as many people are feeling overwhelmed with the demands of the season and the implications of family, good and bad. In my work as a pastor, I have regularly encountered the dual dynamic that the psalmist describes: people who feel abandoned by God even as they search for God, especially as they prepare for the coming of Christ at Christmas. I have also discovered that while "Longest Night" or "Blue Christmas" services are deeply meaningful, many people are reticent to show up for a service with such a specific, difficult theme. The psalmist gives preachers an opportunity to inject some real life into the season: not to take away joy, but to contextualize it. After all, when the psalmist implores God to "let your hand be with the one on your right side—with the one whom you secured as your own," we know with the hindsight of history that the psalmist is describing the church that God has never—and will never—abandon (v. 17).

Bringing the Text to Life

About three years ago, my mother passed away after a long illness. During those difficult last few months, I learned quite a bit about longing and what it can mean. When someone you love suffers so deeply, there is a certain difficult longing for the release of death. You look at the circumstances and think, nothing can cure this but that which comes from God. While no one wants to think about death at Christmas (or, in some cases, ever), few times in life make us feel the sort of desperation the psalmist describes than when a loved one is suffering.

Incidentally, the Advent and Christmas season is a time when painful memories swirl for those who have experienced loss. My mom was a fan of over-the-top Christmas celebrations, and the first Christmas after her death felt like a day we were simply doing our best to endure. Like the psalmist, we felt far from God that Christmas. Perhaps Psalm 80 presents more of an apropos message than it would appear upon first glance.

Ideas for Preaching on Matthew 1:18-25

The last Sunday of Advent can be one of the most difficult Sundays of the year for the preacher, as the church attempts to hold on to one last bit of Advent preparation, while the congregation is itching to get to Christmas. The Gospel passage for Advent 4 invites the preacher to just get over it and let Christ be born.

That said, the focus of this passage isn't on Jesus, but on Joseph, his father. Joseph does not appear very often in scripture, so this level of specificity invites us to pay attention. Matthew is intentional in describing Joseph as "righteous," and the actions presented here surely back up that description. When Joseph first learns of Mary's pregnancy, he plans to quietly break off the engagement, rather than humiliating her. Later, after an angel comes to him in a dream, Joseph follows through with his nuptials, despite the inevitable scuttlebutt among their family and friends.

In the midst of a packed season, Joseph demonstrates two character traits desperately needed in the present day: steadfastness and courage. In a time when being seen as being right is more important than actually being right, Joseph presents a strong rejoinder. What matters is doing the right thing, despite the cost to one's own reputation. This way of being is not flashy, it will not make you famous (the fact of Joseph's inclusion in Holy Scripture notwithstanding!), and it involves a lifetime of faithfulness, day in and day out. It is a way of being, however, entirely consistent with God's plan for the world, and it may well help you keep your head screwed on correctly during one of the busiest seasons of the year.

Joseph's courage is just as important because it takes courage to live this way. It takes courage to make the decision to quietly care for someone you love. It takes courage to follow through with a wedding because of a message you received in a dream. Courage is a vital part of faith, because living out faith requires opening oneself to slings and arrows. Faith requires vulnerability, which is its own kind of courage. Some years ago, Bishop Tom Berlin described the spiritual power of courage this way: "courage is sanctifying grace." If preaching is about helping a person or a congregation grow in faith, then preaching courage—including God's courage at being willing to send Jesus to earth—is necessary to sanctification.

Bringing the Text to Life

- Congregations are full of people who have taken courageous steps in faith. Consider some of the well-known stories of your community and share them, by video, by testimony, or by telling their stories in the sermon.

- Likewise, churches often have long-serving saints who have plugged away at the work of faith for decades. Consider highlighting these people.

- Consider what it means for God to be with us. How can Emmanuel inspire us to courage?

Notes

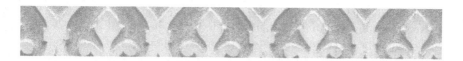

December 24, 2025–
Nativity of the Lord

Isaiah 9:2-7; Psalm 96; Titus 2:11-14; **Luke 2:1-14, (15-20)**

Dalton Rushing

Preacher to Preacher Prayer

O God, You are Wonderful Counselor, Mighty God, Eternal Father, Prince of Peace. You have finally arrived, and not a moment too soon. Thank you for arriving in this very real world to do the very real work of building your kingdom. Help us to linger at the manger, and then send us forth to do your work. Amen.

Ideas for Preaching on Isaiah 9:2-7

Light is such a common biblical metaphor that it has almost lost its power. We hear this metaphor used throughout scripture, in traditional hymnody and modern songs, and in countless sermons. Very practically, evening Christmas Eve worship offers a chance to explore this metaphor in depth for people used to worshipping in the morning. There is a certain Christmas joy that can only be experienced in the dark: Christmas lights, for one, or candlelight singing. Light comes into great focus when darkness surrounds us. If you have ever had a chance to experience complete darkness, as happens inside a deep cave, you will know of light's great power. A single candle can light a whole room.

The writer of Isaiah 9 understands the power of light and dark, and not just as a disconnected metaphor. The writer references the occupation of Israel by the Midianites and the subsequent oppression. One needs to understand the power of darkness to appreciate the even stronger power of light.

Along these lines, the preacher who uses this Old Testament passage to celebrate a New Testament savior has an opportunity to ground the good news of Jesus's birth in the context of the real suffering that is endemic to life. It is because of the memory of oppression that Isaiah's hearers can rejoice. It is because of the continued challenges of life and faith that the coming of the "Wonderful Counselor, Mighty God, Eternal Father, Prince of Peace" carries with it such poetic power (v. 6). It is because of the depth of the dark that the light shines so fiercely.

It is in the midst of this world—not the world as it could be, but the world as it is—that a child is born to us. Authority will be on his shoulders, Isaiah says, which is a helpful thing to remind a people who are so used to feeling as if everything is up to them. Christians have a role to play in the redemption of the world, but the vast authority of God means that we need not feel completely responsible for this gargantuan task. That work has already begun, made manifest in the gift of the Christ child on Christmas.

The darkness is real, and it is awfully dark. But in Bethlehem of Judea, a light shines that is powerful enough to illuminate all the corners of the world.

Bringing the Text to Life

- If the time of the service allows, consider beginning the sermon in darkness. Give flashlights or candles to people around the room to slowly increase the amount of light.

- Share stories of true hardship and the ways in which God has shown up in the midst of such times. There is power in these stories!

- Remind the congregation that even amidst our celebration, there are places in the world that struggle. Invite the congregation to act as mirrors of God's light in those places.

Ideas for Preaching on Luke 2:1-14, (15-20)

Upon the completion of the United States constitution, the American founding father Benjamin Franklin famously proclaimed, "Our new Constitution is now established, and has an appearance that promises permanency; but in this world nothing can be said to be certain, except death and taxes." Joseph and Mary certainly discovered this idiom to be true, as not even Mary's advanced pregnancy prevented them from being forced to travel for many miles to Joseph's hometown of Bethlehem, in order to be added to the census and for the government to tax them.

It is fitting that the story of Jesus's birth begins this way, not merely as it relates to prophecy, but also as it relates to the quotidian nature of the whole ordeal, the sheer every-day-ness that accompanied the arrival of the savior of the world. Jesus showed up in the middle of tax season. He was laid in a manger, a feed trough. He was first visited by shepherds in Luke's account, not royalty, but everyday workers.

The shepherds play a pivotal role in this story, which is to say that according to Luke, they provide the first external signs of Jesus's divinity. Mary and Joseph have had advance notice of who Jesus would be, of course, but Luke tells readers that even so, when the shepherds arrived at the site of Jesus's birth and shared what they had seen, "Everyone who heard it was amazed at what the shepherds told them" (v. 18).

There is, within this story, a clear picture of the intersection of Jesus's humanity and divinity. He was born poor enough to have to find rest in a feeding trough, but his presence was announced by throngs of angels. The fact of his birth is shared not with high royalty in this Gospel, but with lowly shepherds. And yet keeping watch out in their fields, the shepherds did not experience predators but the glory of the Lord.

It can be difficult to imagine oneself in the midst of such a story, so grandly presented each year with nativity plays and beautiful music and all the rest. But the truth of the nativity is not bound by such grandiosity, mostly because it never began with such a thing, God's grand presence notwithstanding. The truth of the nativity owes its power to the presence of God in the everyday, the normal tasks of life. And it reminds us that while death and taxes may be inevitable, in God's world, so is eternal life.

Bringing the Text to Life

Like with all the Advent readings, the preacher has an opportunity to surprise the congregation gathered out of obligation or ritual with a hopeful word. It is precisely in the midst of our obligations and rituals that God shows up. Consider sharing stories of times when something mundane has been interrupted and changed everything.

Christmas Eve and Christmas Day can be difficult times for many people bound by loss or loneliness. Though not necessarily created for this purpose, live-streaming of worship is a lifeline for these people. Consider the ways in which people at home can actively participate with the congregation rather than viewing the service as one would view a television program. Acknowledge those watching the stream and encourage them to sing. Share with them early in the service that you will be lighting candles later, and invite them to participate.

Notes

December 28–Wesleyan Covenant Service for the New Year

2 Kings 23:1-3; Psalm 8; **Ecclesiastes 3:1-13; Matthew 25:31-46***; John 15:1-8;* **Revelation 21:1-6a**

Charley Reeb

The Wesley Covenant Service is a special worship service that occurs just before or at the very beginning of the new year. It provides an opportunity to reflect on the previous year and make a recommitment to God for the new year. Central to the service is the Covenant Prayer, a powerful and profound statement of surrender to God. This service is also called a "Watch Night" service because it often takes place late in the evening on New Year's Eve. John Wesley was particularly fond of this service. It is believed that Wesley celebrated the first Covenant Service in the Methodist Movement on August 11, 1755. This service provides a sacred time to spiritually reset and renew our promise to Christ to be his followers.

For covenant renewal order of service suggestions and other worship resources please visit https://www.umcdiscipleship.org/book-of-worship/covenant-renewal-service.

Preacher to Preacher Prayer

Lord, as we prepare for a new year of ministry put a new and right spirit within us. Prevent us from being distracted by those matters that take time away from the work to which you have called us. Give us patience, understanding and compassion for those we have been entrusted to serve. Open our minds and hearts to different and more creative ways of doing ministry. Stoke the fire within us to proclaim the gospel. Give us the strength to be faithful. Amen.

Ideas for Preaching on Ecclesiastes 3:1-13

This familiar text from Ecclesiastes on the different seasons of life lends itself to a sermon for a covenant renewal service. As folks enter a new year, they are also thinking about beginning a new season in their lives. Listeners will be reflecting on the past year and what they would like to change in the new year. For many, recommitting themselves to Christ through a covenant service is just what the doctor ordered. For some, the past year has been a difficult one and represents a season they would like to see come to a close. What new season is in store for them as they face a new year? How can a recommitment to faith help them meet their goals and prepare them for the next chapter?

Bringing the Text to Life

- Ask worshippers to take five minutes and write done their goals for the new year. Have music playing in the background. You may want to provide journals for the occasion and encourage those in attendance to commit to keeping a prayer journal each day of the new year. Provide a time in the service for worshippers to dedicate their goals to God. Here is a key question to ask as they journal: In what ways is God calling you to grow and serve in the new year?

- Do a "blessing of the calendars." Have everyone lift up all of their time-keepers (watches, cell phones, day planners, etc.) and ask God to be present in all of our days and plans. Commit to be present to God as we plan and live each day.

Ideas for Preaching on Matthew 25:31-46

There will be many attending the covenant renewal service who desire to be more intentional about serving the needy and poor and being generous with their resources in the new year. Perhaps they feel convicted about their lack of generosity and want to change. There is not a better text that speaks to such a conviction than the Parable of the Sheep and Goats. It is the supreme reminder of what should be at the top of our list of priorities as followers of Christ – serving the least of those around us in the same way we would serve Christ himself. In fact, Jesus is clear in this parable that he has such a heart for those who suffer and is so connected to their pain that when we serve the hungry, lonely, and poor we are indeed serving him. We should be looking for the face of Jesus in everyone we serve.

Bringing the Text to Life

- Look up poignant quotes from Mother Theresa that relate to this text.

- Provide copies of Wesley's Covenant Prayer as folks enter worship. This prayer is central to the worship service and a profound commitment to God.

Ideas for Preaching on Revelation 21:1-6a

It's clear why this passage would do well in a covenant renewal service. It is not just a magnificent picture of heaven. It also speaks of God's ability to make all things new. This could be a much-needed word for those who are drawn to this special service. Divorce, death, broken relationships, lost jobs and disappointments will be on the hearts of many in worship. You may also have people who are battling addictions and yearn for the new year to bring them freedom from their enslavement and healing from their brokenness. Lifting up God's power and ability to bring healing and restoration will comfort and encourage those who want to forget the challenges of the last year and focus on the hope and opportunities awaiting them in the new year.

Bringing the Text to Life

- Mention David as someone God restored and made new. He went from a murderer and adulterer to Israel's greatest king. The story of the Apostle Paul is also a good example of God's power of restoration and renewal.

- If there is someone in your congregation who has a moving testimony about being saved and restored by Christ, encourage them to share their story in the service. This will offer hope and encouragement to those who are uncertain about what the new year will bring.

Notes

Notes

January

1. Clyde Edgerton, *Walking Across Egypt* (Ballantine Books, 1989).

2. F. Beckman, *A Man Called Ove* (First Astria Books, 2014); *Home Alone*, directed by Chris Columbus (1990).

3. J. Harader, Living by the Word, *The Christian Century*, 21.

4. L. Kushner, *God Was in This Place and I, I Did Not Know*, 25th anniversary ed. (Jewish Lights Publishing, 2016).

5. Ann Weems, "Stars for the Righteous," in *Putting the Amazing Back in Grace* (Westminster John Knox Press, 1999), 33.

6. General Board of Discipleship, *By Water and the Spirit: A United Methodist Understanding of Baptism*, accessed Sept 7, 2023, https://www.umcdiscipleship.org/resources/by-water-and-the-spirit-full-text

7. "Salt and Light: Salt's Commentary for Epiphany 5," January 30, 2023, Saltproject.org, http s://www.saltproject.org/progressive-christian-blog/2020/2/3/salt-and-light-salts-lectionary-commentary-for-epiphany-5.

8. *Just Mercy*, directed by D. D. Cretton (2019).

9. Martin Luther King, Jr., *Letter from a Birmingham Jail* (Penguin Classics, 2018).

February

1. Drew Hart, *Who Will Be a Witness?* (Harrisonburg: Herald Press, 2020).

2. *Ted Lasso*, episode 3, Trent Crimm: The Independent, retrieved from Lassoism.com: https://lassoism.com/Ted-Lasso-S01E03-trent-crimm-the-independent.php.

3. Christoper Hall, *A Different Way: Recentering the Christian Life Around Following Jesus.* (HarperCollins, 2023).

4. *The Book of Discipline of The United Methodist Church* (The United Methodist Publishing House, 2016), ¶ 330.

5. Hall, *A Different Way.*

6. Dictionary.com, s.v. "kind," accessed Oct 29, 2023, https://www.dictionary.com/browse/kind.

March

1. Nolan L. Cabrera (2022, October 2). "Activism or Slacktivism? The Potential and Pitfalls of Social Media in Contemporary Student Activism," *Academia*, October 2, 2022, https://www.academia.edu/34753295.

2. Lois Tverberg, "Levav—Heart, Mind," *En-Gedi Resource Center*, July 1, 2015, https://engediresourcecenter.com/2015/07/01/levav-heart-mind/.

3. Clayton Childers, "Rethinking Lent," *United Methodist Insight*, March 25, 2022, https://um-insight.net/perspectives/rethinking-lent/. See also John Schwiebert's response to Childers' article.

4. Ronald Rolheiser, "Entering Lent," *Ron Rolheiser, OMI*, February 22, 2009, from https://ronrolheiser.com/entering-lent/.

5. Pádraig Ó Tuama, *In the Shelter: Finding a Home in the World.* (1517 Media, 2015), 201.

6. D. Hayward, *Eraser Jesus*, print, *Naked Pastor*, accessed August 24, 2023, https://nakedpastor.com/products/eraser-poster.

7. Scott Erickson, *Trinity Hug*, print, *Scott Erickson Art Shop.* accessed September 6, 2023, https://scotterricksonartshop.com/collections/prints/products/trinity-hug.

8. Scott Erickson, *Trinity Hug, Instagram*, accessed September 6, 2023, https://www.instagram.com/p/Cwu-imlLuqw/

9. Kelly Latimore, *Christ: The Mother Hen*, April 21, 222, print, *Kelly Latimore Icons*, accessed September 1, 2023, https://kellylatimoreicons.com/blogs/news/christ-the-mother-hen.

10. D. Brown, "How One Man Convinced 200 Ku Klux Klan Members to Give Up Their Robes," *NPR*, August 20, 2017, https://www.npr.org/2017/08/20/544861933/how-one-man-convinced-200-ku-klux-klan-members-to-give-up-their-robes.

11. "Mother hens 'can feel their chicks' pain'," *Al Bawaba (Middle East) Ltd.*, accessed August 29, 2023, https://www.thefreelibrary.com/Mother+hens+'can+feel+their+chicks'+pain'.-a0251104710.

12. Diana Sanchez, ed., *The Hymns of the United Methodist Hymnal: Introduction to the Hymns, Canticles, and Acts of Worship* (Abingdon Press, 1989), 291.

13. Brother Lawrence, *The Practice of the Presence of God* (Spire Books, 1967), 30.

14. Brene Brown, *The Gifts of Imperfection: 10th Anniversary Edition: Features a New Foreword and Brand-new Tools* (Hazelden Publishing, 2022), 56–57.

15. Wendy Francisco, "GOD AND DOG," *YouTube*, accessed September 1, 2023, https://www.youtube.com/watch?v=c7ZkSm24xiM.

16. The Tariq Khamisa Foundation (TKF), accessed September 7, 2023, https://www.tkf.org/?fbclid=IwAR2k_HKQJ99-sx_yRq7DG8CoDAApUM k3yKe5hSMkEBI0f59FkN6vKlsI2wA.

April

1. See https://www.npr.org/sections/thetwo-way/2013/03/28/175601237/in -ritual-pope-francis-washes-the-feet-of-young-inmates-women.

2. See https://youtu.be/Nz4gshe7jQE.

3. John Chrysostom, "On the Crucifixion of Christ."

4. Dick Wills, *Waking to God's Dream: Spiritual Leadership and Church Renewal* (Nashville: Abingdon, 1999), 67.

5. Hugh T. McElrath and Bill J. Leonard, *Becoming Christian: Dimensions of Spiritual Formation*, ed. Bill J. Leonard (Westminster/John Knox Press, 1990), 54.

May

1. Marguerite Ward, "This Princeton professor posted his CV of failures for the world to see," *CNBC*, April 27, 2016, https://www.cnbc.com/2016/04/27/this -princeton-professor-posted-his-cv-of-failures-for-the-world-to-see.html.

2. Warren G. Bennis and Burt Nanus, *Leaders: Strategies for Taking Charge*, 2nd ed. (HarperBusiness Essentials, 2003), 70.

3. Philip Yancey, *The Jesus I Never Knew* (Zondervan, 1995), 182–83.

4. Kent Struckmeyer, *A Conspiracy of Love: Following Jesus in Postmodern World* (Resource, 2016), 190.

5. M. Robert Mulholland, Jr., "The Longest Victory," in *Journey Through the Bible: Revelation* (Cokesbury, 1996).

August

1. Rick, Noack, "The climate crisis could be behind French vineyard devastation as April frosts loom," *The Independent*, May 2, 2021, https://www.independent .co.uk/life-style/food-and-drink/french-vineyards-frost-climate-b1838269.html.

2. Mary Oliver, "Backyard," *Owls and Other Fantasies, Poems and Essays* (Beacon Press, 2003).

3. Maria Pasquini, "American Runner Helps Competitor to Finish Line After Falling: 'My Version of Trying to Be a Hero,'" *People Magazine*, August 2, 2021, https://people.com/sports/tokyo-olympics-american-runner-helps-competitor-to -finish-line-after-falling/.

4. See https://emilypost.com/advice/seating-at-an-official-luncheon-or-dinner.

October

1. "G4982 - Sōzō - Strong's Greek Lexicon (KJV)," *Blue Letter Bible*, accessed August 21, 2023, https://www.blueletterbible.org/lexicon/g4982/kjv/tr/0-1/.

2. Walter Brueggemann, *Jeremiah* (William B. Eerdmans Publishing Company, 1998), 291.

3. "Love Divine, All Loves Excelling," *The United Methodist Hymnal: Book of United Methodist Worship* (The United Methodist Publishing House, 1989), 384.

4. Martin Luther King, Jr., "Remaining Awake Through a Great Revolution," speech given at the National Cathedral, March 31, 1968, https://iu.pressbooks.pub/phstp105/chapter/rev-dr-martin-luther-king-jr/.

5. Frederick Buechner, *Wishful Thinking: A Seeker's ABC* (HarperSanFrancisco, 1993).

November

1. "And Are We Yet Alive," *The United Methodist Hymnal: Book of United Methodist Worship* (The United Methodist Publishing House, 1989), 553.

2. Francis Bacon, *The Oxford Francis Bacon, Vol. 4: The Advancement of Learning*, ed. Michael Kiernan (Oxford University Press, 2000), no. 1, https://www.preachingtoday.com/illustrations/1996/december/435.html.

Contributors

Rachel Cornwell
July 27, August 3, August 10, August 17, August 24, August 31

Hugh Hendrickson
May 18, May 25, June 1, June 8, June 15

Chris Jones
April 27, May 4, May 11

Pam McCurdy
June 22, June 29, July 6

Cyndi McDonald
January 5, January 12, January 19, January 26, February 2

Sarah B. Miller
October 12, October 19, October 26, November 2, November 9

Charley Reeb
September 7, September 14, September 21, September 28, October 5, December 28

Dalton Rushing
November 30, December 7, December 14, December 21, December 24

Chelsea Simon
March 5, March 9, March 16, March 23, March 30

Cynthia D. Weems
February 9, February 16, February 23, March 2

Andy Whitaker-Smith
November 16, November 23, November 27

Jennifer Wyant
April 6, April 13, April 17, April 18, April 20

Lisa Yebuah
July 13, July 20

Online Edition

The Abingdon Preaching Annual 2025 online edition is available by subscription at www.ministrymatters.com.

Abingdon Press is pleased to make available an online edition of *The Abingdon Preaching Annual 2025* as part of our Ministry Matters online community and resources.

Subscribers to our online edition will also have access to preaching content from prior years.

Visit www.ministrymatters.com and click on SUBSCRIBE NOW. From that menu, select "Abingdon Preaching Annual" and follow the prompt to set up an account.

Please note, your subscription to the Abingdon Preaching Annual will be renewed automatically, unless you contact MinistryMatters.com to request a change.

Scripture Index

Old Testament

New Testament

The Apocrypha

Sirach

Be prepared at a moment's notice

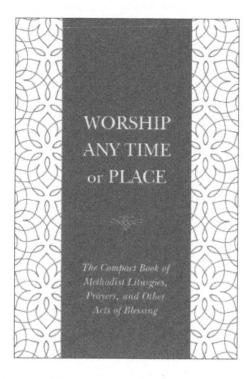

From pulpits to pews, from altar tables to dinner tables, from sanctuaries to streets, *Worship Any Time or Place* is a compact guide that equips the Methodist pastor, worship leader, or layperson to create meaningful worship moments for any group of people, any time, any place.

It includes liturgies and prayers suitable for traditional settings such as worship services, funeral services, and administration of the sacraments, plus words to use during hospital visits, retreats, church meetings, and other conventional settings, and more.

9781791029838 Print
9781791029845 eBook

Published by
Abingdon Press

800-672-1789 | Cokesbury.com

Made in the USA
Monee, IL
19 September 2024

66160738R00125